NUTSHELLS

"A" LEVEL LAW
IN A NUTSHELL

Other Titles in the Series

Company Law
Constitutional and Administrative Law
Consumer Law
Contract
Criminal Law
European Law
Family Law
Land Law
Tort
Trusts

AUSTRALIA
LBC Information Service
Sydney

CANADA AND U.S.A.
Carswell
Toronto

NEW ZEALAND
Brooker's
Auckland

SINGAPORE AND MALAYSIA
Thompson Information (S.E. Asia)
Singapore

NUTSHELLS

"A" LEVEL LAW
IN A NUTSHELL

FIRST EDITION

by

MARTIN HUNT
Course Manager: Legal Studies,
Stanmore College

London • Sweet & Maxwell • 1997

Published in 1996 by Sweet & Maxwell Limited of
100 Avenue Road, London NW3 3PF
Computerset by Wyvern Typesetting Ltd, Bristol
Printed in England by Clays Ltd, St Ives plc

No natural forests were destroyed to make this product; only farmed
timber was used and replanted.

A CIP Catalogue record for this book is available from the British Library

ISBN 0–421–58880-2

CONTENTS

Section One:
THE LAW-MAKING PROCESS

Introduction

English law is made up of a number of different sources (or types) of law, which fall into two main categories: legislative sources, consisting of primary legislation (or Acts of Parliament), delegated (or secondary) legislation and European legislation; judicial sources, consisting of common law (legal principles developed by the courts) and Equity. There are also a number of minor sources, such as custom and the writings of legal academics. In addition to considering the major sources identified above, any examination of the law-making process must also include discussion of statutory interpretation (the way in which the courts interpret and apply Acts of Parliament).

Prior to examining these major sources in detail, it is useful to reflect on the reasons for this variety of laws. The law is required to perform a wide range of functions in society and the legal system has to use a number of different techniques to achieve this. No one form of law-making would be able to cope with this variety of demands, as each has particular advantages and is suited to particular tasks. It may help to imagine English law as a large wall protecting society: the bricks being made of Acts of Parliament, European Regulations, etc. with the common law as the mortar, binding the whole system together. These various sources complement, rather than compete, with each other ensuring English law continues to develop in response to changing social and economic demands.

1. PRIMARY LEGISLATION

The importance of Acts of Parliament

Acts of Parliament (as the term 'primary' above indicates) are the highest form of law in England. All other sources either derive their validity from, or are subordinate to, Acts of Parliament: powers to make delegated legislation are granted in enabling Acts; European Union law is incorporated into English law by the European Communities Act 1972; common law and Equity are both subordinate to legislation—where there is conflict, legislation prevails.

The reason for this is principally constitutional. Under England's unwritten constitution, Parliament is sovereign. Therefore, its enacted will, in the form of Acts of Parliament, cannot be challenged in the courts. There are, of course, practical political limitations on the ways in which Parliament exercises its sovereignty. Membership of the European Union has also imposed limits on Parliament's theoretically absolute sovereignty.

Given their sovereign status, together with the fact that they deal with the most fundamental questions of social and economic policy, it is essential that the process by which Acts of Parliament are made is efficient (in that it produces new legislation promptly when required), effective (in that it produces legislation of sufficient technical quality), and democratic (in that all interested and affected parties have an opportunity to participate).

Sources of legislative proposals

Proposals for new Acts of Parliament come from a number of sources, the most important being: the Government; advisory agencies; pressure groups; and individual Members of Parliament. New legislation may also result from an initiative by the European Union to give effect to international treaty obligations, or in response to prompting by the courts.

The Government: most new Acts of Parliament are introduced by the Government. Some of these may be as a result of pledges made in an election manifesto. Others, such as Finance Acts, must be passed whichever political party is in power. Some legislation may be passed in response to an unexpected emergency, for example, the Prevention of Terrorism (Temporary Provisions) Act 1974. However, most Government legislation results from discussions in Cabinet while in power. As the government is democratically elected, is well-informed, and is served by a large number of highly qualified and experienced advisors, this would seem to comply with the requirements of efficiency, effectiveness and democracy.

Advisory Agencies: a large number of proposals come from the various advisory committees and commissions established to advise the Government. These agencies may be either standing (or permanent) bodies or *ad hoc* (or temporary) bodies. The most important standing agency is the Law Commission. This was established in 1966 with a brief to keep all areas of the law under constant review and produce a systematic programme of law reform. In addition to bringing about a number of significant reforms, the Law Commission plays an important role in stimulating debate about the state of the law. However, the Commission has recently expressed concern that, due to insufficient parliamentary consideration of its reports, much of its work is wasted. *Ad hoc* agencies (such as Royal Commissions) are established to investigate a particular issue of concern and are disbanded once they have reported. The use of such agencies, with their high degree of expertise, can only serve to enhance the efficiency and effectiveness of the legislative process. Furthermore, the extensive consultation they undertake makes an important contribution to the democratic nature of that process.

Pressure Groups: a pressure group is any group which seeks to influence the legislative process by organised lobbying. This includes not only 'cause' groups, such as CND and Greenpeace, but also 'sectional' groups, such as the CBI and TUC. The role of such groups has increased dramatically in recent years, as more people have become involved in this type of organisation rather than in the traditional political parties.

The activities of pressure groups bring a number of benefits to the legislative process. They can inform and assist the Legislature on the need for new legislation and the form it should take, thereby improving the efficiency and effectiveness of the process. They also inform and stimulate public debate. Furthermore, by bringing people together collectively and involving them in the process, they can empower the naturally weaker groups in society. This all contributes to the democratic nature of the procedure.

However, there are potential disadvantages associated with pressure group activity. A group which is well-organised and resourced may be able to achieve a degree of influence out of all proportion to its size and to the level of support it enjoys in society at large. This danger has increased with the growth of professional lobbying agencies and the number of M.P.s acting as consultants to such organisations. There is, therefore, a risk that pressure group activity may distort, rather than enhance, the democratic quality of the process.

Nevertheless, pressure group activity is inevitable and, in many respects, beneficial. Therefore, what is required is a system of regulation in order to prevent any abuse of influence. Recently, measures have been introduced to achieve this following the report of the Nolan Committee on Standards in Public Life.

Individual M.P.s: a certain amount of parliamentary time is reserved for discussion of proposals put forward by individual M.P.s, known as Private Members' Bills. These are often based upon suggestions by pressure groups or recommendations from an advisory agency. Most successful Private Members' Bills are uncontroversial and of a minor and technical nature. This is largely because the Government can use its control of the parliamentary timetable to block any Bill it opposes. Nevertheless, some major and controversial legislation has come about in this way, for example, the Murder (Abolition of the Death Penalty) Act 1965 and the Abortion Act 1967. The most important feature of Private Members' Bills is that they ensure that the legislative process is not dominated entirely by the Government.

Consultation

Once the Government has adopted a proposal for new legislation, a consultation period follows. This involves issuing a discussion document in the form of either a Green Paper or a White Paper. A Green Paper is used to announce tentative proposals for discussion, while a White Paper announces firm Government policy for implementation. The opportunity for consultation is essential to the efficient, effective and democratic nature of the process, as it allows interested parties to comment on the desirability of the proposals and to point out any technical defects or contradictions.

Drafting

Following the consultation period, the proposal must be translated into draft legislation, known as a Bill. All Government Bills are drafted by expert civil servants in the Office of Parliamentary Counsel. While perfection in drafting is inevitably unobtainable, concerns have been expressed that growth in the volume of legislation, together with its increasing complexity, has led to a decline in its technical quality. Suggestions for improvement, such as that by Dale for the establishment of a Law Council to review the technical quality of draft legislation, have not been implemented. Nevertheless, it seems clear that some reform is required in order to ensure efficiency and effectiveness.

Enactment

For a Bill to become an Act of Parliament, it must pass through the process of enactment in both Houses of Parliament. While a Bill may be introduced first into either House, most important or controversial Bills commence in the House of Commons. The various stages in the process of enactment are as follows:

First Reading: the title of the Bill is announced to the House. This is a purely formal stage with no debate or vote.

Second Reading: this is a general debate on the main principles and purpose of the Bill. If more than twenty M.P.s wish to object to the Bill, there is a vote.

Committee Stage: this is arguably the most important stage, as it is at this point that the Bill is debated in detail, clause by clause. This is normally done by a Standing Committee, though it may also be done by the appropriate Select Committee or by the full House sitting as a Committee. At this stage the Bill may be amended. This sharing out of Bills allows them to proceed more quickly, thereby improving efficiency.

Report Stage: this is when the Committee reports its proceedings to the full House. Any amendments made in Committee will be either accepted or reversed. Further amendments may also be made.

Third Reading: this is a further general debate on the Bill in its final, amended form. Only minor, technical amendments are allowed.

The Bill then proceeds to the other House, where this process is repeated. Any further amendments are referred back to the originating House for consideration. The House of Commons can reject the House of Lords' amendments.

Once the Bill has passed successfully through both Houses, it proceeds for Royal Assent, which is, again, a purely formal stage. Upon receipt of Royal Assent, the Bill becomes an Act of Parliament. The provisions of the Act will then come into force immediately; upon a date specified in the Act itself; or upon the issuing of a Commencement Order by the appropriate minister.

This may appear a rather slow and cumbersome procedure. However, it is important that Bills dealing with major questions of social and economic policy receive adequate scrutiny and debate before becoming law. Nevertheless, a Government with a secure majority is able to ensure its proposals are enacted without significant alteration or amendment.

2. DELEGATED LEGISLATION

Introduction

Delegated legislation is law made by certain individuals and institutions acting under a grant of legislative power from Parliament. These powers are generally granted in an enabling Act, which establishes a framework of general principles and gives powers to others to fill in the details. Thus, there are two important distinctions between primary and delegated legislation:

(a) while Parliament's legislative power is unlimited, the powers of the delegated legislator are limited and defined by the enabling Act;

(b) while primary legislation cannot be challenged in the courts (as there are no grounds on which to declare it unconstitutional), delegated legislation is subject to judicial review.

There are three main forms of delegated legislation:

Statutory Instruments: these are rules, regulations and orders issued by ministers and are national in effect.

Byelaws: these are generally issued by local authorities and are local in effect, limited to the jurisdiction of the council concerned. Some state corporations also have the power to issue byelaws.

Orders in Council: these are issued by the Privy Council and are generally only used in emergencies.

The reasons for delegated legislation

There are four main reasons for the use of delegated legislation:

To save parliamentary time: Due to the limited time available, Parliament could not enact all the detailed rules and regulations required by a modern society. The use of delegated legislation to deal with the details leaves Parliament free to concentrate on debating and deciding major policy issues.

Enhances Efficiency

To deal with complex and technical issues: much modern legislation is very complex and technical, e.g. health and safety regulations, so the use of delegated legislation allows experts in the relevant field to become involved, thus enhancing the effectiveness of the regulations.

Enhances effectiveness

To enable prompt amendments to the law: in order to keep up with social and technological change, the law must be frequently amended and updated. Amending an Act of Parliament is too long and complicated to meet this challenge. By contrast, it is much easier and quicker to amend delegated legislation. This also means that delegated legislation can be used to respond quickly to emergencies.

To allow for local variation: the power of local authorities to issue byelaws allows for local variations that may be necessary to meet specific needs.

Thus, the use of delegated legislation is both inevitable and beneficial in any modern state. However, delegated legislation is the result of transferring important legislative powers from Parliament (the Legislature) to national and local government (the Executive). This means there must be an effective system of checks and controls over the use of delegated powers to ensure that they are used properly and accountably.

Checks and controls over the use of delegated powers

There are three main forms of check and control over the use of delegated powers:

Consultation: it is common for the enabling Act to require the person who has been granted powers to consult before exercising them. The Act may specify who must be consulted or may merely require reasonable consultation. Even where consultation is not mandatory, it generally takes place as a matter of routine. This acts as a check on the use of the power in two ways:

(a) **directly:** by requiring public exercise of the power;

(b) **indirectly:** by forming the basis for a possible judicial challenge.

Parliamentary oversight: this may seem to conflict with the need to save parliamentary time. However, a responsible Parliament must use some of the time it has saved by delegating powers to monitor their use. This is achieved in two ways:

(a) **the affirmation process:** most statutory instruments must be affirmed (or approved) before coming into force. This may involve positive affirmation where the instrument does not come into force unless approved by a positive resolution in Parliament. The more common procedure, however, is negative affirmation, where the instrument comes into force unless annulled by a negative resolution in Parliament. This reliance on negative affirmation raises the danger that new instruments receive inadequate policy review. The Hansard Society has recommended that this be improved by referring draft instruments to the appropriate departmental select committee for policy review prior to affirmation.

(b) **the Joint Select Committee on Statutory Instruments:** this is a parliamentary committee with the task of reviewing the technical merits of draft instruments and referring to Parliament any which give cause for concern. Grounds for referring an instrument include where there is some doubt as to whether it is *intra vires* (within the power) or where it makes an unusual or unexpected use of the power. Therefore, the committee acts as a filter so that Parliament need only take time to consider the small proportion of instruments which are referred to it.

Parliament may also amend or revoke the grant of power if this proves to be necessary.

Judicial review: the basis of the courts' authority to review the validity of delegated legislation lies in the limited nature of the delegated powers. Therefore, the courts can annul delegated legislation where it is found to be *ultra vires* (outside or beyond the power). There are two forms of *ultra vires*:

(a) **Substantive *ultra vires:*** this is where the subject matter of the legislation is outside the scope of the enabling power (*Attorney General v. Fulham Corporation* (1921));

(b) **procedural *ultra vires:*** this is where the subject matter of the legislation is within the scope of the enabling power but there has been a serious failure to comply with a mandatory procedural requirement, e.g., a failure to consult (*Agricultural Training Board v. Aylesbury Mushrooms Ltd* (1972)).

3. ENGLISH LAW AND THE EUROPEAN UNION

Introduction

At the end of World War II, there was a strong desire among the Western European nations for political and economic cooperation. It was hoped that this would not only help with postwar physical and economic reconstruction, but also that the resulting interdependency of nations would prevent any future conflict. This led to the establishment of the European Coal and Steel Community in 1952, followed by the European Economic Community and European Atomic Energy Community in 1958. These communities merged in 1965, and are now known as the European Union.

At first, Britain was not a member of these communities, preferring to rely on its links with the Commonwealth, the 'special relationship' with the USA, and a leading role in the European Free Trade Association. However, as the success of the communities became clear, Britain applied to join, first in 1961 and again in 1967. A third, successful application was made in 1970 and Britain became a member of the communities on January 1, 1973.

The main original aims of the European Union were to promote the economic development of the member states and improve the living standards of their citizens. These have since been expanded to include environmental policy, social policy, and monetary and political union. In order to achieve these aims, the Union has had to establish its own legal institutions and laws: a European legal order. It is this legal order, and its relationship to the English legal system, that must now be considered.

The institutions of the European Union

There are five major institutions:

The European Council: this was established in 1974 and consists of the heads of government and foreign ministers of the member states. It is this body that takes major decisions on the future of the Union at 'Euro-Summits'.

The Council of Ministers: this is the main decision-making and legislative body of the Union. It consists of ministers from the governments of the Member States, and is advised by the Committee of Permanent Representatives (composed of civil servants from the Member States). It is this body that adopts (enacts) most Union legislation following proposals put to it by the Commission.

The Commission: this is the main executive body of the Union. It is headed by the President of the Commission and is divided into a number of Directorates-General (similar to United Kingdom ministries). Each Directorate is headed by a Commissioner. The President and the Commissioners are nominated by the Member States but act independently, as it is their role to represent the collective interest of the Union. The Commission is responsible for the administration of the Union; it also proposes most Union legislation to the Council of Ministers and has minor legislative powers of its own.

The Parliament: this is mainly a consultative and advisory body and, therefore, should not be thought of as being similar to the United Kingdom Parliament. Its members are directly elected from each Member State and sit in political, rather than national, groupings.

The Court of Justice: the jurisdiction of the Court is essentially two-fold:
    (a) as an administrative court, it deals with actions against Member States and Union institutions. It also reviews the validity of Union legislation. Under Article 173 of the Treaty of Rome, it can annul Union legislation on four grounds:
        (i) lack of competence (similar to substantive *ultra vires*);
        (ii) infringement of an essential procedural requirement (similar to procedural *ultra vires*);
        (iii) infringement of the Treaty (*i.e.* as unconstitutional);
        (iv) misuse of power.

(b) as a constitutional court, it provides definitive interpretations of Union law, including the Treaties. In doing this the
Court uses a purposive approach, seeking to advance the
purpose behind the law.

The relationship between the Court of Justice and the national
courts of the Member States will be discussed below. Since 1989,
the Court of Justice has been assisted by a Court of First Instance.
This court deals with many of the routine administrative cases,
leaving the Court of Justice free to concentrate on its constitutional
role.

The Court consists of judges nominated by the member states.
In addition to hearing argument from the parties to a case, the
Court also receives an advisory opinion from an Advocate-General.
The Court then delivers a single judgment. While not strictly
bound to follow its own previous decisions, in practice the Court
will only depart from them in exceptional circumstances.

Direct applicability and direct effect

Before considering the different forms of Union law, it is important
to understand two central concepts of the European legal order:

(a) **direct applicability:** a provision of Union law is directly
applicable where it *automatically* forms part of the national law
of each Member State. There is no need for the Member States
to take national action to implement it.

(b) **direct effect:** a provision of Union law is directly effective
where it creates individual rights enforceable in national
courts. There are two forms of direct effect:
  (i) **vertical direct effect:** this creates individual rights
  against the state;
  (ii) **horizontal direct effect:** this creates individual rights
  against other individuals.

These notions have important consequences for the sovereignty of
the United Kingdom Parliament, which will be discussed below.

The sources of European Union law

The Treaties: these are the primary source of Union law. They outline the aims and principles of the Union, establish and empower its institutions, and provide for the introduction of Union legislation. Therefore, they may be regarded as the constitution of the Union. Provisions of the Treaties are *not* directly applicable. The Court of Justice has held that they may have both vertical and horizontal direct effect where they are clear, precise and unconditional (*Van Gend en Loos v. Nederlandse Administratie der Belastingen (1963)*).

Union legislation: legislation under Article 189 of the Treaty of Rome is the secondary souce of Union law. Under Article 189, there are three forms of Union legislation:

(a) **Regulations:** these are directly applicable. They are binding in their entirety and, therefore, cannot be varied or amended by national legislation. Thus, they create legislative *uniformity* throughout the Union. Regulations can have both vertical and horizontal direct effect where the *Van Gend* requirements are met (*Leonesio v. Italian Ministry of Agriculture (1973)*).

(b) **Directives:** these are *not* directly applicable. They are binding as to the result to be achieved, but leave the choice of the form and method of implementation to each Member State (in the United Kingdom this is usually done through delegated legislation). Therefore, they create legislative *harmony* throughout the Union. Directives may have vertical direct effect *provided* the *Van Gend* requirements are met (*Van Duyn v. Home Office* (1974)) and the time limit specified for national implementation has expired (*Marshall v. Southampton and South-West Hampshire Area Health Authority* (1986)). Thus, while an individual may be able to rely on a Directive against the state, they cannot do so against another individual. However, in the latter circumstance, the individual may still have a remedy against the state where three conditions are met (*Francovitch and others v. Italy (1993)*):

(i) the purpose of the Directive was to create individual rights;

(ii) those rights are specified precisely in the Directive;

(iii) there is a causal link between the failure of the Member State to implement the Directive and the damage suffered by the individual.

(c) Decisions: these are *not* directly applicable. They are binding in their entirety upon those to whom they are addressed. They may be addressed to Member States, companies and, exceptionally, individuals. A Decision may have vertical direct effect *provided* the *Van Gend* requirements are met and *provided* it is addressed to a Member State (*Grad v. Finanzamt Traunstein (1970)*).

Union membership and the sovereignty of Parliament

The Union has, because of the potential for direct applicability and direct effect of its legislation, the power to make laws which automatically form part of English law and which can create individual rights that the English courts must enforce.

This raises the question of sovereignty, because it is necessary to decide which law, European or English, will prevail where they conflict. In order to resolve this question both the European and United Kingdom view must be considered:

The European view: this is quite clear. The Court of Justice has stated that if the objectives of the Union are to be achieved, European law must prevail over inconsistent national law. Member States have, therefore, by joining the Union, permanently transferred part of their sovereignty to it (*Costa v. ENEL* (1964)). National courts must, in cases of conflict, give priority to European law and set aside the inconsistent national law (*Minister of Finance v. Simmenthal* (1978)).

The United Kingdom view: this is less straightforward. Section 2(1) of the European Communities Act 1972 incorporates European law into English law and provides, where appropriate, for the direct applicability and direct effect of that law. There is, therefore, by virtue of section 2(1), a potential conflict between the United Kingdom's Union obligations under the 1972 Act and the traditional sovereignty of Parliament.

Section 2(4) of the 1972 Act enacts a modified version of the *Costa* position, by stating that all United Kingdom legislation takes effect subject to European law *with the exception* of the 1972 Act itself. This would seem to allow Parliament to restore the primacy of United Kingdom legislation by amending or repealing section 2: it is an 'escape clause' from the permanency of the position taken by the Court of Justice in *Costa*. This, together with subsequent case law, would indicate the following position:

(a) the English courts will attempt to resolve any inconsistency between European and English law through interpretation; *i.e.* they will interpret the English law in such a way as to make it consistent with European law unless expressly instructed by Parliament to do otherwise (*Garland v. British Rail Engineering Ltd* (1982)).

(b) if Parliament wishes to enact legislation contrary to European law, it must repeal or amend section 2. In the absence of any such express instruction to do otherwise, the English courts will give effect to European law, and disapply the inconsistent English legislation (*Macarthys Ltd v. Smith* (1979)).

(c) in exceptional circumstances, the English courts may suspend the operation of English legislation pending guidance from the Court of Justice regarding an apparent inconsistency (*R v. Secretary of State for Transport*, ex p. *Factortame Ltd and others (No. 2)* (1990)).

(d) there has, therefore, been a limited and temporary suspension of sovereignty, albeit for an unlimited period. Parliament retains, by virtue of section 2(4), a residual power to re-assert its full sovereignty by repealing or amending section 2. However, as this would mean the United Kingdom was repudiating its membership of the Union, it seems unlikely that this would ever be done. In practice, therefore, the transfer or pooling of sovereignty would seem to be permanent.

The United Kingdom courts and the Court of Justice

One of the main functions of the Court of Justice is to give definitive interpretations of European law. It does this in response to questions referred to it by national courts for a preliminary ruling. The national court will then decide the case in light of the ruling from the Court of Justice. This emphasises that while it is the Court of Justice that interprets European law, it is the national courts of the Member States that apply it.

Under Article 177 of the Treaty of Rome, any national court *may* request a ruling where it is necessary to enable it to give judgment; *i.e.* where the disputed point of European law is material to the decision, the national court has a discretion to refer that point to the Court of Justice. Where the national court is one from which there is no appeal (in the United Kingdom, this would be the House of Lords), then it has no choice; where a ruling is necessary to enable it to give judgment, it *must* make a reference.

In deciding whether a ruling is necessary to enable it to give judgment, the English courts make use of the guidelines established in *Bulmer v. Bollinger* (1974), e.g., a ruling is *not* necessary where the Court of Justice has previously given a ruling on the point in question (*i.e.* the point may be resolved by reference to the case law of the Court of Justice) or where the point is reasonably clear and free from doubt (the *acte clair* doctrine).

4. STATUTORY INTERPRETATION Nov-Dec '98

Introduction

Interpretation is an inevitable aspect of any form of communication. It is the interpretation placed upon information which gives it meaning. Problems arise where someone misinterprets information or where different people arrive at different interpretations of the same information. Zander (*The Law-Making Process*, 4th ed., Butterworths) has identified three reasons why legislation is likely to suffer from these problems:

(a) it tends to be complicated and is often a mixture of ordinary and technical language.

(b) it is often concerned with regulating future conduct. As the ability of the draftsman to anticipate the future is inevitably limited, problems will arise as to whether a particular provision applies to a particular case.

(c) it is often concerned with regulating competing interests (for example, employer and employee, landlord and tenant, trader and consumer) where the people concerned have a self-interest in promoting different interpretations.

While it is for Parliament (or those delegated by Parliament) to make legislation, it is the courts who provide the definitive interpretation when any of these problems arise.

Judicial approaches to interpretation

There are three traditional approaches (sometimes referred to as rules or canons) to the interpretation of statutes:

(a) **the literal approach:** here, the courts should give the disputed words their ordinary, literal meaning, regardless of the outcome. If the outcome is absurd or repugnant, the remedy lies in parliamentary amendment, not judicial interpretation (*R v. Judge of the City of London Court* (1892)).

(b) **the golden approach:** here, the courts should give the disputed words their ordinary, literal meaning *unless* the outcome is absurd or repugnant, in which case a more appropriate alternative interpretation may be used (*Grey v. Pearson* (1857)).

(c) **the mischief (or modern purposive) approach:** here, the court should give the disputed words the interpretation most likely to promote the purpose behind the legislation. Therefore, the court consider not only the words themselves but also what Parliament intended them to achieve (*Heydon's Case* (1584); *Re Attorney General's Reference (No. 1)* (1988)). Nevertheless, even under a purposive approach, the starting point for interpretation must remain the actual words used by Parliament (*Black-Clawson International Ltd v. Papierwerk Waldhof-Aschaffenburg AG* (1975)). This is essential to preserve the proper constitutional balance between Parliament as the makers of legislation and the courts as its interpreters.

In recent years, the courts have developed an approach to interpretation which combines elements of all three of the traditional approaches: the modern unitary approach. Under this approach, the courts must respect the actual words of the provision but, rather than adhere strictly to their literal meaning, should interpret them having regard to the context in which they are used and the purpose underlying the provision in which they appear. Of these three elements (words, context and purpose), it is the purposive which has become increasingly decisive (*Carter v. Bradbeer* (1975); *Pepper (Inspector of Taxes v. Hart and others* (1993)), a tendency due, in part, to the increasing influence of the European Court of Justice.

Subsidiary principles and presumptions of interpretation

The courts are also guided in the interpretation of legislation by a number of minor principles and presumptions. Among the more significant are two rules of language:

(a) **the *ejusdem generis* principle:** where general words follow a list of specific words, the general take their meaning from the specific. For example, a provision referring to 'cats, dogs and other animals' would apply to domestic animals only, not to wild animals or livestock.

(b) **the *expressio unius exclusio alterius* principle:** the express inclusion of one member of a particular class excludes, by implication, all others not included. For example, a provision referring to 'quarries and coal mines' would apply to all types of quarry and to coal mines, but not to any other type of mine.

Among the more significant presumptions are the presumption against retrospective effect, and the presumption of *mens rea* in criminal statutes.

An analysis of the three main elements

(a) **the literal element:** there are three main arguments for emphasising the literal element:

(i) it promotes certainty;
(ii) it reduces litigation;
(iii) it is constitutionally correct.

However, there are also arguments against it:

(i) it ignores the natural ambiguity of language. Words rarely have one, single literal meaning. The correct meaning can only be decided by reference to the context in which the word is used. Therefore, there is frequently uncertainty which has to be resolved by the courts.

(ii) it fails to take account of the inevitable imperfection of draftsmanship.

(iii) it is an automatic and unthinking response. The literal interpretation may often be the correct one, but it is not automatically so.

Therefore, it would be undesirable for the courts to over-emphasise the literal meaning of the disputed words.

(b) **the contextual (or golden) element:** this at least avoids the most absurd or repugnant consequences of over-emphasising the literal meaning. However, it is unclear precisely what degree of absurdity or repugnance is required to justify the court abandoning the literal meaning. Therefore, according to Zander, it is an 'unpredictable safety valve' which 'cannot be regarded as a sound basis for judicial decision making' (Michael Zander, *The Law-Making Process*, 4th ed. Butterworths, at p. 130).

(c) **the purposive element:** this acknowledges the various factors which give rise to problems of interpretation and that the courts should seek to resolve them by arriving at the interpretation most likely to achieve the purpose of the legislation. This is clearly the most desirable approach for the courts to take and, therefore, the present emphasis on the purposive element within a unitary approach represents the most satisfactory balance of these three elements.

However, there is a major obstacle to effective purposive interpretation. There are significant restrictions on the range of materials available to the courts to help them identify the purpose of the legislation. These materials fall into two categories:

(a) **intrinsic aids to interpretation:** this is information within the statute itself. The courts can take into account:
  (i) the long and short titles;
  (ii) the preamble;
  (iii) the headings;
  (iv) the schedules.
but they may not make reference to the marginal notes.

(b) **extrinsic aids to interpretation:** this is information outside the statute. The courts can make reference to:
  (i) other statutes;
  (ii) official government publications directly related to its enactment (for example, Green or White Papers, Law Commission reports), but only to identify the defect in the previous law, not the remedy the new law was intended to provide (the 'Black-Clawson' rule);
  (iii) where the legislation is related to an international treaty or convention, the treaty of convention itself (*Salomon v. Commissioners of Customs and Excise* (1967));
  (iv) the official record of parliamentary debates and proceedings (Hansard), but only in limited and exceptional circumstances (*Pepper (Inspector of Taxes) v. Hart and others* (1993)).
The court may not refer to:
  (i) any official publication not directly related to the enactment of the statute
  (ii) unofficial publications (for example, pressure group reports)
The restrictions on the materials available, particularly regarding extrinsic aids, can make it difficult for the court to identify the precise purpose of the legislation. The Law Commission, in a 1969 report, made a number of recommendations to remedy this:
  (a) that the marginal notes should be available to the courts;
  (b) that official documents be available to identify not only the defect, but also the remedy;
  (c) that an explanatory memorandum be attached to the statute for the guidance of the courts. This would be a combination of three existing documents:
    (i) the preamble;
    (ii) the explanatory document prepared for M.P.s;
    (iii) the detailed briefings prepared for ministers.
Unfortunately, these recommendations have not been implemented.

5. PRECEDENT

Introduction

The English legal system is a common law system. This means that many of its laws have developed over time through decisions of the courts. Before the Norman Conquest, there was no 'English' law as such. Rather, there was a variety of different regional systems. This was unacceptable to the new Norman rulers who were great centralisers and administrators. Therefore, Henry II sent his judges around the country on 'circuits' and gradually established a single system of law for the whole country: a common law. It was this process that first established the importance of judicial decisions as a source of law, though it was not truly formalised until the establishment of a reliable system of case reporting in 1865 and the restructuring of the courts under the Judicature Acts 1873–1875.

The basis of the doctrine of precedent is the principle of *stare decisis* (or, more correctly, *stare rationibus decidendis*). This requires that a later court be bound to apply the same reasoning as an earlier court where the two cases raise substantially the same questions of principle. This development of the law according to established principles is the hallmark of judicial law-making, as contrasted with development according to policy by the legislature. It is legislative evolution rather than legislative revolution. The reasoning behind such an approach is clear: it satisfies a basic requirement of justice, that similar cases be decided according to similar principles. It also ensures that judicial decisions are based on reason and principle, not on arbitrary, individualised factors.

In order to operate a doctrine of binding precedent, the legal system must have three essential elements:

(a) **a hierarchy of courts:** to establish which decisions are binding on which courts.

The basic principle here is that the decisions of higher courts are binding on lower courts. The highest court in the English system is the House of Lords. Decisions of the House of Lords are binding on all lower civil and criminal courts. It is not itself bound by the decisions of any court *except* the Court of Justice of the European Union on matters of Union law *alone*. The next most authoritative court is the Court of Appeal. This has two divisions; civil and criminal. Decisions of the Civil Division are binding on all lower civil courts, while those of the Criminal Division bind all lower criminal courts.

Below the Court of Appeal are the Divisional Courts, the High Court, the Crown Court, the county court and the magistrates' court. While both the Divisional Courts and the High Court can establish precedents, in practice the great majority of common law is to be found in decisions of the House of Lords and Court of Appeal.

(b) an accurate system of law reporting: to allow this body of principle to be identified, collated and accessed.

The earliest form of law reporting was the Year Books, first published in 1272. Modern reporting dates from the establishment of the Council on Law Reporting in 1865 (which became the Incorporated Council in 1870). The Council still publishes the Law Reports and, since 1953, the Weekly Law Reports. Various private companies also publish both general and specialised series of reports, the best known being the All England Law Reports (published by Butterworths). Reports are also published in various newspapers (for example, The Times) and journals (for example, the New Law Journal). The most recent development in this field has been the introduction of computerised reporting systems (such as LEXIS).

(c) a set of principles to identify the binding element in a decision.

A judgment will generally contain four elements:
  (i) a statement of the material (or relevant) facts of the case;
  (ii) a statement of the legal principles material to the decision (known as the *ratio decidendi*).
  (iii) discussion of legal principles raised in argument but not material to the decision (known as *obiter dicta*);
  (iv) the decision or verdict.

It is the *ratio*, and the *ratio* alone, which forms the binding element upon future courts when dealing with cases of a similar nature.

The *obiter dicta*, while never binding, may have a strong persuasive force in future cases. Other forms of persuasive precedent include decisions of the Privy Council, decisions of other common law jurisdiction (notably Australia, Canada and New Zealand), and the writings of legal academics.

③ Flexibility and certainty in precedent

The common law faces a dilemma between the competing but equally legitimate aims of flexibility and certainty. The law needs to be flexible in order to develop and evolve to meet changing times and demands. It must also be sufficiently certain to allow people to plan their affairs and lawyers to advise their clients. The binding nature of the *ratio* clearly creates a foundation of certainty. It is necessary to consider, therefore, the mechanisms by which a degree of flexibility is introduced into the system:

(a) **overruling, reversing and disapproving:** a higher court can always alter the law as developed by a lower court. Where this is done on appeal, it is known as reversing. When it occurs where the lower decision is being cited as authority in another case, it is known as overruling. A case can only be overruled where its *ratio* is material to the decision in the later case. Where it is not material, the higher court can only disapprove the decision of the lower court. A case which has been disapproved, while in strict terms still a valid precedent, is unlikely to be cited successfully in the future.

(b) **distinguishing:** a lower court may be able to avoid following the *ratio* of a higher court where it can distinguish between the two cases. It is in this way that exceptions to the general principles are developed. To distinguish means to find some material difference between the two cases which justifies the application of different principles. However, this discretion to distinguish may be misused by a lower court in order to avoid an unwelcome precedent. This practice is clearly unacceptable

and was condemned by the Court of Appeal in *Lewis v. Averay*
(1972).

(c) **departing:** the notion of departing refers to the circumstances under which a court can depart from *its own* previous
decisions. Until 1966, the House of Lords was bound by its own
previous decisions (*London Tramways v. London County Council*
(1898)). This created a block at the top of the system of precedent, and meant that out-dated, incorrect or unacceptable
decisions could only be rectified by legislation. Therefore, in
1966, the Lord Chancellor issued a *Practice Statement* which
stated that while the House of Lords would regard its own previous decisions as normally binding, it would depart from them
when it appeared right to do so. In exercising this discretion,
the House of Lords is required to take into account:

   (i) the danger of disturbing retrospectively existing civil
       arrangements;
   (ii) the particular need for certainty in the criminal law.

The Court of Appeal (Civil Division) is normally bound by its own
previous decisions, *subject to* the exceptions established in *Young v.
Bristol Aeroplane Co Ltd* (1944). For example, it is not bound where
the previous decision was given *per incuriam*. This means that the
decision was given in ignorance or forgetfulness of relevant legislation or of a decision by the House of Lords, with the result that
the decision is demonstrably wrong (*Morelle v. Wakeling* (1955); *Duke
v. Reliance Systems Ltd* (1988)).

   The Court of Appeal (Criminal Division) is similarly bound by
its own previous decisions subject to the *Bristol Aeroplane* exceptions
and to the exception established in *R v. Taylor* (1950): it is not bound
where, in the previous decision, the law was misapplied or misun-
derstood resulting in a conviction and, therefore, to follow it would
result in a manifest injustice. The Criminal Division has this additional element of flexibility because it is dealing with questions
affecting the liberty of the citizen.

 ## An analysis of the operation of precedent

The operation of a doctrine of binding precedent has a number of
advantages:

(a) it is a just system, ensuring that similar cases are decided by similar principles;

(b) it is an impartial system, requiring decisions to be made according to established principles;

(c) it provides a practical character to the law, allowing it to develop in response to actual cases, rather than on an exclusively theoretical or abstract basis;

(d) it provides a degree of certainty, allowing individuals to order their affairs and lawyers to advise their clients;

(e) it allows a measure of flexibility, in that within the binding framework of *stare decisis*, the hierarchy of courts, the appellate process, the provisions of the Practice Statement, the *Bristol Aeroplane* and *R v. Taylor* exceptions and the practice of distinguishing, allow the common law to develop and evolve to meet changing needs and times.

However, there are also **disadvantages**:

(a) there is a danger of rigidity, whereby necessary changes cannot occur because:

 (i) the system is contingent—change are dependent upon an appropriate case reaching a sufficiently superior court (this is sometimes referred to as the accidents of litigation);

 (ii) the retrospective effect of overruling can discourage the court from changing the law.

(b) it is a complex system:

 (i) keeping track of valid authorities and the exceptions established through distinguishing is a very difficult task.

 (ii) it can be difficult to identify the precise *ratio* of a decision, particularly where it is contained in the multiple judgements of the House of Lords and Court of Appeal.

There are two possible reforms which could enhance the flexibility of the system without significantly reducing the present level of certainty:

(a) public interest referrals: at present, necessary changes may be delayed because individual litigants may be unwilling or unable to commit the time and money involved to taking their case to the superior courts. A public interest referral system would allow the trial judge to refer questions of law of general public importance to the superior courts, at public expense. This process would operate in a very similar fashion to Article 177 references to the Court of Justice of the European Union.

(b) **prospective overruling:** at present, a court may be discouraged from overruling because of the retrospective consequences of such action. Indeed, the House of Lords is specifically required to bear this in mind under the Practice Statement. Under prospective overruling, any retrospective effect would be limited to the instant case and any similar case where proceedings had already commenced.

6. EQUITY Jan'99

Introduction

Equity is a system of rules and principles which operates alongside the common law. Its function is to supplement the common law and to remedy any hardship arising from the strict application of common law rules. For this reason, Equity is often referred to as a 'gloss' on the common law. Equity is concerned with ensuring fairness and justice by granting the courts a degree of discretion in order to avoid instances of formal injustice. Therefore, fairness and discretion may be seen as the essence of Equity. Accordingly, its rules and remedies will not be applied where this would itself result in hardship or injustice (for example, where legitimate third party rights are involved). This can also be seen in many of the maxims of Equity: for example, 'he who seeks Equity must do Equity'; 'he who comes to Equity must come with clean hands'; 'delay defeats Equity'.

The historical emergence and development of Equity

Equity emerged in response to problems with the operation of the common law:

(a) **technical problems with the writ system:** to commence an action at common law, the plaintiff had to issue the correct writ from those listed by the Chancery. If he selected the wrong one or made a technical error in its drafting, his action would fail. Furthermore, by the end of the thirteenth century, the ability of the Chancery to develop new writs was severely limited.

(b) **reliance of the common law on a single remedy: damages:** plaintiffs often found damages to be an inadequate or inappropriate remedy. Equity was able to develop a range of alternative, discretionary remedies, such as specific performance and injunctions.

(c) **the limited nature of common law rights:** for example, the common law did not recognise the transfer of property from one person (A) to another (B) for the benefit of a third (C). Under common law, B's ownership was absolute and his obligations to C unenforceable. Equity developed the notion of the trust to protect C's beneficial interest in the property.

Faced with these difficulties, individuals began to petition the Lord Chancellor, and the Court of Chancery evolved to deal with these cases. Thus, over time, and particularly during the seventeenth and eighteenth centuries, Equity developed as a separate system of rules and principles operating alongside the common law.

However, by the nineteenth century, this dual system of law and Equity was itself causing problems. In particular, litigation was subject to long delays and had become extremely expensive. As a result, there was a major reorganisation of the court structure under the Judicature Acts 1873–1875. This involved the *procedural* fusion of law and Equity. From this point, all courts had both common law and Equitable jurisdiction. Regarding the *substantive* relationship between the two systems, the *Earl of Oxford's Case* (1615) had established that where there was conflict, Equity should prevail. This was confirmed by section 25(11) of the 1873 Act. Thus, the two systems (as opposed to jurisdictions) remained distinct, the continuing discretionary nature of Equity being the clearest evidence of this.

The modern nature and significance of Equity

In the early part of the twentieth century, concerns were expressed that Equity had stagnated, and that it had fallen victim to the very faults of rigidity and formality that it had evolved to remedy. It may be that such a development was to some extent inevitable. There is an inherent tendency in any legal system towards formality. Similar concerns have been expressed regarding the tribunal system. Any decline in the innovatory capacity of Equity may also be due to a modern preference for legislative rather than judicial development, and an increasing reliance on formal methods of law reform rather than judicial creativity.

These concerns led Lord Denning, in 1952, to call for a 'new Equity', and the subsequent years have seen a re-emergence of judicial confidence in their law-making role, and of what Lord Devlin has termed 'judicial activism'. In fact, there is ample evidence in recent years of the continuing vitality of Equity:

(a) **Equitable estoppel:** this is where a person may be held to a promise, even where it is not made under seal or as part of a contract (*Central London Property Trust Ltd v. High Trees House Ltd* (1947)).

(b) **Anton Piller orders:** these are injunctions which prevent the removal, concealment or destruction of evidence in the defendant's possession (*Anton Piller KG v. Manufacturing Processes Ltd* (1976)).

(c) **Mareva injunctions:** these are injunctions which prevent the removal of assets by the defendant from the jurisdiction of the English courts (*Mareva Compania Naviera SA v. International Bulkcarriers SA* (1975)).

There have also been important developments in other areas of Equity (for example, in relation to constructive trusts) and it should be noted that older inventions of Equity (such as the trust) remain just as important today.

Section Two: PERSONNEL AND PROCEDURES

1. THE COURT AND APPELLATE SYSTEM

The House of Lords

Staff: the Lord Chancellor presides over the House of Lords, assisted by the Lords of Appeal in Ordinary (the Law Lords) and any other peer who has held high judicial office. It must sit with at least three members, though the usual practice is to sit as a court of five members, each of whom is entitled to deliver an 'opinion'.

Jurisdiction: the House of Lords has little remaining original jurisdiction (for example, disputed peerage claims) and is now almost exclusively concerned with hearing appeals. Though it has full civil and criminal jurisdiction, in practice it is primarily concerned with civil business.

The Court of Appeal

Staff: the Civil Division is presided over by the Master of the Rolls and the Criminal Division by the Lord Chief Justice. They are assisted by the President of the Family Division of the High Court, the Vice-Chancellor and the Lords Justices of Appeal. It may also call on any High Court judge to sit. It normally sits as a court of three, though in exceptionally important cases it may sit as a court of five or seven. In the Civil Division, each member is entitled to deliver a judgment whereas in the Criminal Division, there is usually a single judgment delivered by the presiding judge. This is to prevent uncertainty arising in the criminal law from dissenting judgments.

Jurisdiction: the Court of Appeal has exclusively appellate jurisdiction.

The High Court

Staff: the High Court consists of three divisions: Queen's Bench; Chancery; and Family. The Queen's Bench Division is presided over by the Lord Chief Justice, the Chancery Division by the Vice-Chancellor, and the Family Division by the President. They are assisted by the High Court (or puisne) judges. Each division may sit with a judge alone as a Division of the High Court, or with two or more judges as a Divisional Court. The distinction between these two formats is one of jurisdiction.

Jurisdiction:
(a) The High Court (Queen's Bench Division) has original civil jurisdiction (principally regarding large value claims in contract and tort). It may also sit as a Commercial Court, an Admiralty Court and an Election Court.

(b) The Queen's Bench Divisional Court deals with the judicial review of administrative action, in which the validity of actions by the state can be challenged by affected individuals. It also hears applications for the writ of *habeas corpus* and exercises appellate criminal jurisdiction, hearing appeals by way of case stated from the magistrates' court or from the magistrates' court via the Crown Court.

(c) The High Court (Chancery Division) has original jurisdiction over land matters, trusts, contentious probate, company, partnership and bankruptcy matters, and intellectual property. It also hears appeals from the county court over taxation and insolvency. It may also sit as a Patents Court.

(d) The Chancery Divisional Court hears appeals regarding taxation and land registration.

(e) The High Court (Family Division) has original jurisdiction over matrimonial matters, family matters (including issues relating to children) and non-contentious probate.

(f) The Family Divisional Court hears appeals regarding family matters from the magistrates' court.

The Crown Court

Staff: cases will be heard by either a High Court judge, circuit judge, recorder or assistant recorder, depending on the gravity of the offence concerned.

Jurisdiction: the Crown Court has exclusive original jurisdiction over criminal offences tried on indictment (the most serious offences) and also hears cases involving triable-either-way offences (less serious offences) where the defendant has elected to be tried on indictment. It also hears appeals from summary conviction (for minor offences) in the magistrates courts. It also has minor civil appellate jurisdiction (most notably regarding licensing appeals from the magistrates' court).

The County Court

Staff: cases in the County Court are heard by Circuit Judges and District Judges (formerly known as Registrars). The judge may be assisted by lay assessors (defined by the Courts and Legal Services Act 1990, section 14 as persons 'of skill and experience in the matter to which the proceedings relate').

Jurisdiction: the County Court has exclusively original civil jurisdiction. This principally involves lesser value claims in contract and tort, together with some equity and probate matters. Some County Courts are also designated divorce county courts that hear undefended divorce cases.

The County Court Small Claims Arbitration Procedure

This scheme, introduced by the Administration of Justice Act 1973, is one of the most important aspects of the work of the County Court. Proceedings involving claims of £3,000 or less are automatically referred to arbitration. Cases involving larger sums can also use the arbitration scheme if the parties agree.

The arbitration hearing is usually before a District Judge. The proceedings are far less formal than a full trial, allowing the District Judge to play a more active, inquisitorial role. This is clearly necessary in proceedings which are intended to allow people to present their own case without the need for professional representation.

Regarding representation, while professional representation is permitted, costs cannot be recovered from the losing party. This 'no costs' rule is designed to discourage the use of lawyers and preserve informality. Alternatively, the parties may be assisted by a 'friend', though the 'friend' may only address the proceedings with the leave of the District Judge.

The scheme has proved to be both successful and popular. The Civil Justice Review (1988) found a high degree of satisfaction among users of the scheme. There are, however, two problems:

(a) too many people are unaware of the scheme and, therefore, are still deterred from pursuing their rights through fear of lengthy and expensive litigation.

(b) successful claimants often experience difficulties in enforcing judgment (the Civil Justice Review found that approximately 25 per cent of successful claimants had not received the compensation ordered by the court). There needs to be a simple, low-cost enforcement process to operate alongside the arbitration scheme itself.

The magistrates' court

Staff: these courts are staffed primarily by lay magistrates, though the busier metropolitan areas also use professional magistrates (known as stipendiaries). Lay magistrates sit as a bench of three, while a stipendiary magistrate sits alone.

Jurisdiction:

(a) *Civil*: the magistrates' court has a small amount of civil jurisdiction over minor family matters, some forms of civil debt (such as non-payment of Council Tax) and the granting of licences (for taxis, public houses, *etc.*).

(b) *Criminal*: the criminal jurisdiction of the magistrates' court falls into two elements:

(i) as a summary court to deal with minor criminal offences or offences that can be tried either way where the defendant has elected to be tried summarily (together these form approximately 95 per cent of criminal trials). The magistrates have limited sentencing powers. Where they are of the opinion that the offence merits a more severe sentence, the magistrates can commit the offender for sentencing at the Crown Court.

When dealing with young offenders (formerly known as juveniles), specially trained magistrates sit as a youth court (with different procedures and powers).

   (ii) as examining magistrates in committal proceedings. This arises where the accused has been charged with an indictable offence or an offence that can be tried either way and elected for trial on indictment. The purpose of the proceedings is not to decide guilt or innocence, but to determine whether the accused has a case to answer. Where the magistrates are of the view that there is a case to answer, the accused will be committed for trial at the Crown Court. Where they are not, the accused will be discharged.

Appeals in civil proceedings: Appeals from the magistrates' court in licensing matters go to the Crown Court, and in family matters to the High Court (Family Division).

Appeals from the County Court in insolvency proceedings lie to the High Court (Chancery Division). Appeals from the arbitration scheme lie to the full County Court. In all other matters, appeal (on either a point of law or point of fact) lies to the Court of Appeal (Civil Division). Generally, such an appeal lies as of right (*i.e.* no leave (permission) is required). However, for small value claims the leave of the Court of Appeal is required.

Appeals from the High Court lie to the Court of Appeal (Civil Division). Generally, leave is not required. However, under the *leapfrog* procedure in the Administration of Justice Act 1969, direct appeal to the House of Lords is possible if two requirements are met:

   (a) the trial judge must grant a certificate of satisfaction, stating that the parties agree to the procedure and that the case involves a point of law of general public importance which is either:
      (i) concerned wholly or partly with the interpretation of an Act of Parliament or Statutory Instrument;
      (ii) is one on which the trial judge is bound by a previous decision of the Court of Appeal or House of Lords.
   (b) the House of Lords grants leave to appeal.

Appeals from the Court of Appeal (Civil Division) lie to the House of Lords. The leave of either court is required. In civil appeals, there is no statutory requirement that the appeal involve a point of law of general public importance. In practice, however, leave is unlikely to be granted unless the appeal discloses an 'arguable point of law of general public importance' (Procedure Direction (1988)).

Appeals in criminal proceedings following summary trial

Appeal from the magistrates' court lie to either:
  (a) the Crown Court. Where the accused pleaded guilty, he can only appeal against sentence. Where the plea was one of not guilty, he may appeal against conviction, sentence or both. The Crown Court can confirm, reverse or vary the decision of the magistrates (including increasing the sentence). Further appeal on a point of law can be made by either the defence or prosecution to the Queen's Bench Divisional Court by way of case stated.
  (b) alternatively, either the defence or prosecution can appeal directly, by way of case stated, from the magistrates' court to the Queen's Bench Divisional Court. The Divisional Court can confirm, reverse or vary the decision of the magistrates or remit the case back to the magistrates' court with its opinion.

Further appeal lies from the Divisional Court to the House of Lords *provided* two requirements are met (Administration of Justice Act 1960, s.1):
  (a) the Divisional Court must certify that the appeal raises a point of law of general public importance.
  (b) either the Divisional Court or the House of Lords must grant leave on the basis that the point of law is one which ought to be considered by the House of Lords.

Appeals in criminal proceedings following trial on indictment

Appeal from the Crown Court to the Court of Appeal (Criminal Division) on a point of law lies as of right. Appeal on a point of fact or mixed point of fact and law is only possible where either:
  (a) the trial judge grants an appeal certificate; or
  (b) the Court of Appeal grants leave.

Unlike appeals following summary trial, a defendant convicted following trial on indictment can appeal against sentence, conviction or both, regardless of the plea entered at trial.

When dealing with an appeal against conviction only, the Court of Appeal has no power to interfere with the sentence passed by the Crown Court. The Court of Appeal must allow an appeal against conviction where it is satisfied either (Criminal Appeal Act 1968, s.2):

(a) that the conviction is unsafe or unsatisfactory; or
(b) that the trial judge had made an error of law; or
(c) that there was a material irregularity in the conduct of the trial.

However, the Court of Appeal has a discretion (known as the *proviso*) to dismiss the appeal, even though satisfied on one or more of these points, where it is of the opinion that no miscarriage of justice has occurred. Where the appeal is allowed, the court can quash the conviction or, in the interests of justice, order a re-trial (Criminal Appeal Act 1968, s.7).

An appeal against sentence is only possible where either:

(a) the trial judge grants an appeal certificate; or
(b) the Court of Appeal grants leave.

The Court of Appeal may confirm, vary or reduce the sentence imposed by the Crown Court—it has no power to increase the sentence. It may also use the opportunity to provide sentencing guidelines for the Crown Court.

Further appeal, by either the defence or prosecution, lies from the Court of Appeal to the House of Lords *provided* two requirements are met (Criminal Appeal Act 1968, s.33):

(a) the Court of Appeal must certify that the appeal raises a point of law of general public importance.
(b) either the Court of Appeal or House of Lords must grant leave on the basis that the point of law is one which ought to be considered by the House of Lords.

While the prosecution cannot appeal against an acquittal, the Attorney-General can refer questions on a point of law to the Court of Appeal (Criminal Justice Act 1972, s.36). The opinion of the Court of Appeal has no effect on the acquittal. Nevertheless, this is an important additional mechanism for resolving doubtful points of criminal law.

Furthermore, while the prosecution cannot appeal against sentence, the Attorney-General may refer the sentence to the Court of Appeal where it is thought to be unduly lenient (Criminal Justice Act 1988, s.36). The Court of Appeal may then confirm, vary,

THE CIVIL COURT STRUCTURE

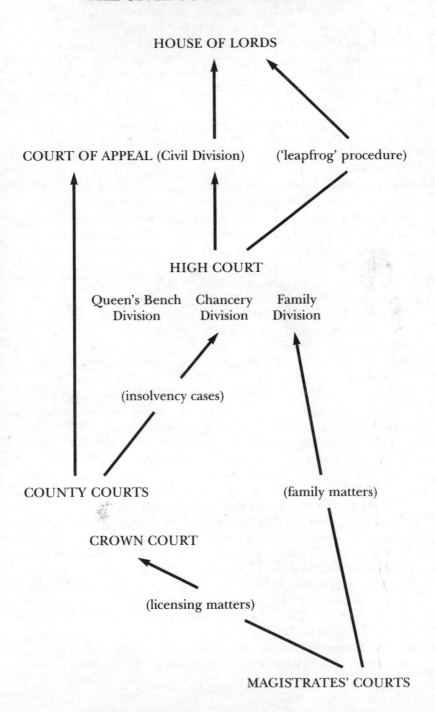

HOUSE OF LORDS

COURT OF APPEAL (Civil Division)   ('leapfrog' procedure)

HIGH COURT

Queen's Bench   Chancery   Family
Division   Division   Division

(insolvency cases)

COUNTY COURTS   (family matters)

CROWN COURT

(licensing matters)

MAGISTRATES' COURTS

decrease or increase the sentence, and may again use the opportunity to issue sentencing guidelines.

2. ALTERNATIVE DISPUTE RESOLUTION

Introduction

Many disputes are resolved informally, for example, through negotiation. However, where an informal approach is unsuccessful or inappropriate, formal mechanisms must be available to ensure the dispute is resolved fairly. The traditional mechanism is the court system. However, for a variety of reasons, the courts themselves are not always the most suitable or appropriate method. It is for this reason that a range of alternative mechanisms have been developed.

Limitations of the courts

There are a number of factors which limit the suitability of the courts as a mechanism for resolving disputes:

(a) **cost:** using the courts is very expensive, both for the individuals concerned and for society as a whole. Furthermore, this expense may not be justified by the value of the dispute.

(b) **delay:** court proceedings are very time consuming and many disputes need a much more urgent solution.

(c) **inaccessibility:** in addition to the factors of cost and delay, many people (particularly those from the least-advantaged sections of society) find the courts intimidating and inaccessible.

(d) **inappropriateness:** the adversarial nature of court proceedings is often inappropriate for the type of dispute; for

THE CRIMINAL COURT STRUCTURE
(SUMMARY TRIALS)

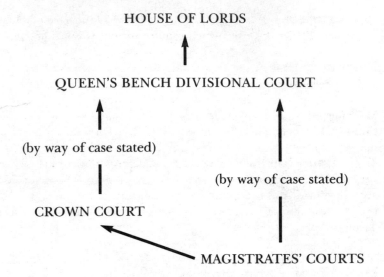

HOUSE OF LORDS

QUEEN'S BENCH DIVISIONAL COURT

(by way of case stated)

(by way of case stated)

CROWN COURT

MAGISTRATES' COURTS

THE CRIMINAL COURT STRUCTURE
(TRIAL ON INDICTMENT)

HOUSE OF LORDS

COURT OF APPEAL (Criminal Division)

CROWN COURT

MAGISTRATES' COURTS
(Committal proceedings)

example, family and matrimonial disputes, especially where children are involved.

(e) **incapacity:** the court system simply could not cope efficiently with all the disputes which require formal resolution.

Nevertheless, the court still performs a valuable role, both in resolving those disputes suitable for any of the alternatives (for example, criminal cases) and in supervising the work of the alternative mechanisms.

The main forms of alternative dispute resolution

(a) Tribunals

There are two forms of tribunal:

Administrative tribunals: administrative (or public) tribunals are designed to deliver justice quickly, cheaply, and with the minimum of formality. While the large number of tribunals makes it difficult to generalise, certain common characteristics can be identified:

(a) all administrative tribunals are created by statute.
(b) a tribunal will usually have three members: a legally-qualified chair and two lay experts.
(c) tribunal members can usually only be dismissed with the consent of the Lord Chancellor. This is an essential safeguard against executive interference in the independence of the tribunal.
(d) procedures are kept as informal as possible. However, some tribunals, such as the Mental Health Review Tribunal, have to be quite formal.
(e) the caseload of different tribunals varies widely. Some (such as the Social Security Appeals Tribunal) deal with thousands of cases each year, while others (for example, the Plant Varieties and Seeds Tribunal) deal with only one or two.
(f) appeal on a point of law can generally be made to the High Court.
(g) tribunals are subject to the supervisory jurisdiction of the Queen's Bench Divisional Court via judicial review.
(h) the work of tribunals is also monitored by the Council on

Tribunals (established in 1958), which delivers an annual report to Parliament.

Domestic tribunals: domestic (or private) tribunals are concerned with the discipline of members of a particular profession or organisation (for example, doctors, solicitors). They are subject to the same rules of natural justice and fair procedure as administrative tribunals. There may also be specific provision for appeals to the courts (for example, to the Privy Council from the General Medical Council).

Advantages: there are five main advantages to the use of tribunals:

(a) **cost:** tribunal proceedings are inexpensive, both in absolute terms and relative to the cost of court proceedings.

(b) **speed:** proceedings are quicker than court proceedings. This also helps to minimise cost.

(c) **informality:** proceedings are kept as informal as possible. This makes them less intimidating than court proceedings and, hence, more accessible.

(d) **expertise:** lay members are appointed for their expertise in the area to which the tribunal relates. The specific jurisdiction of the tribunal develops this expertise further and helps to ensure consistency.

(e) **capacity:** tribunals, which deal with approximately 250,000 cases each year, relieve the courts of an otherwise unmanageable burden.

Disadvantages: there are three potential disadvantages to the use of tribunals:

(a) **poor quality decision-making:** the speed and informality of tribunal proceedings creates a risk of poor quality decision-making. However, this is guarded against through the requirements of fair procedure and natural justice, supervision by the courts, and monitoring by the Council on Tribunals.

(b) **bias:** there is a risk that the use of experts may create a bias against the inexpert claimant. However, this is again met by the safeguards outlined above and the requirement of balance in the membership of many tribunals (for example, industrial tribunals).

(c) **representation:** this is a more significant problem. While professional representation is permitted before most tribunals, legal aid is rarely available. Although an increased use of lawyers runs a risk of increased formality, it is hard to avoid the conclusion that representation should be available equally to all.

(b) Arbitration

Arbitration is the reference of a dispute to an independent third party for determination. The arbitrator (often a member of the Chartered Institute of Arbitrators) makes a decision known as an 'award'. While arbitration is essentially a private arrangement, it is subject to the supervisory jurisdiction of the courts and regulated by statute. There are three areas where the use of arbitration is particularly common:

(a) **Commercial arbitration:** many commercial contracts contain an arbitration clause. This avoids the cost, time and bad feeling that is often involved in litigation, and which could damage future business relationships. It is also a private arrangement which protects commercially sensitive information.

(b) **Industrial arbitration:** arbitration is frequently used to resolve industrial disputes. The Advisory Conciliation and Arbitration Service (established by the Employment Protection

Act 1975) offers a specialised service to disputing parties. This
is a voluntary process whereby the decision of the arbitrator is
not legally binding. However, once the parties have committed
themselves to the process they are unlikely to reject the
decision.

(c) **Consumer arbitration:** many trade associations (such as
ABTA), in conjunction with the Office of Fair Trading, operate
codes of practice which include arbitration schemes. These
offer consumers an attractive low-cost alternative to court proceedings. However, these schemes have three main failings:

  (i) many consumers are unaware that they exist;
 (ii) the association has limited sanctions against any trader
      who breaches the code;
(iii) those traders most likely to cause problems are also
      those least likely to subscribe to a code of practice.

The courts themselves also offer an arbitration service in the
County Courts for small claims of £3,000 or less.

Advantages: arbitration shares many of the advantages of tribunals: cost, speed, informality, expertise. It also has the additional
advantages of privacy (as noted above in relation to commercial
arbitration) and convenience (the arbitration takes place at a time
and place to suit the convenience of the parties).

Disadvantages: the potential disadvantages of poor quality
decision-making and bias are again safeguarded against through
the framework of judicial and statutory regulation, and the fre-
quent use of professional arbitrators.

(c) Inquiries

An inquiry is often used to resolve issues of general public or environmental concern; for example, accident inquiries and planning
inquiries. However, the length of time and cost involved limits their
usefulness as an alternative to the courts. They are a highly specialised mechanism for dealing with very specific issues.

(d) The Ombudsman

The Ombudsman (or 'grievance-man') is an independent official responsible for investigating complaints of maladministration or inefficiency. This concept (which originated in Scandinavia) was first used in Britain in 1967 with the introduction of an ombudsman for central government (the Parliamentary Commissioner for Administration). Public ombudsmen followed for both local government and the National Health Service. The Courts and Legal Services Act 1990 introduced ombudsmen for both legal services and conveyancing. The private sector has also used this concept, particularly in the financial services sector. As it is the only mechanism for investigating complaints, not of wrongs *per se*, but of inefficiency or poor administration, the ombudsman is a valuable addition to the range of alternatives available.

(e) Advice and guidance

It may be argued that the consumer of the services of these various dispute resolution mechanisms is not given adequate guidance in choosing the one most appropriate to their needs. In some parts of the USA a 'multi-door' courthouse approach is used. Here, a person with a dispute is seen first by an 'intake specialist' who advises them on the best method to use. Given that the local courthouse is not the focus of the community in Britain that it is in the USA, this is a service that might be best performed here by the Citizens Advice Bureaux.

3. THE LEGAL PROFESSION

Introduction

The legal profession in England and Wales is divided into two branches: barristers and solicitors. In general terms, the barrister may be thought of as the legal consultant and the solicitor as the legal general practitioner. Solicitors are also often assisted in their work by legal executives.

Barristers

Work and organisation: there are currently approximately 8,400 practising barristers, the vast majority based in London. The governing body of this branch of the profession is the General Council of the Bar (the Bar Council). The most visible aspect of the barrister's work is advocacy (the presentation of a case in court). However, barristers specialising in some areas of the law (for example, revenue law) rarely appear in court. Barristers also deal with a considerable amount of pre-trial paperwork (especially in civil cases), and in giving 'opinions' (a considered view of the merits of a case). They will also spend time in conferences with solicitors and clients.

Training and career: the Bar is largely a graduate profession. The graduate entrant is required to take a one-year vocational course (with an emphasis on skills) organised by the Bar Council. This is followed by a further year of training (known as pupillage) with a qualified and experienced barrister. The trainee must also join one of the four Inns of Court (Gray's Inn, Lincoln's Inn, Inner Temple and Middle Temple) and, largely for reasons of tradition, attend a certain number of dinners during training.

Having completed their training, the newly-qualified barrister must find a place in chambers from which to practice. Chambers is a set of offices from which a group of barristers practice (though they remain self-employed), sharing the running costs and the services of a clerk (who negotiates fees and allocates work). However, vacancies in chambers are limited, and in recent years some new barristers have had to accept unofficial residence as 'squatters' or 'floaters'.

Once qualified, the barrister will be known as a 'junior' and will remain so throughout his career unless promoted to the ranks of Queen's Counsel (Q.C. or 'Silk'). This is an honorific title awarded by the Queen on the advice of the Lord Chancellor. For the barrister, the title means higher fees and an increased chance of becoming a judge. It is also said to be an indication of the most experienced and able barristers. However, as no interview or examination is held it is difficult to regard it as a reliable indicator. Most barristers remain self-employed, though some do go into employment in both the private and public sectors.

Solicitors

Work and organisation: this is the larger of the two branches, there being approximately 66,000 practising solicitors in England

and Wales in 1995. The governing body of this branch of the profession is the Law Society. In addition to self-regulation by the Bar Council and Law Society, the Courts and Legal Services Act 1990 established a new regulatory body for the profession as a whole: the Lord Chancellor's Advisory Committee on Legal Education and Conduct. The solicitor's work involves giving general advice and the administration of clients' legal affairs. A 1985 Law Society survey found that 70 per cent of solicitors' gross fees came from conveyancing, commercial, matrimonial and probate work. Solicitors are also engaged in advocacy, in fact almost all advocacy in the magistrates' courts is undertaken by solicitors and the barristers' monopoly of rights of audience in the higher courts was abolished by the 1990 Act.

Training and career: as with the Bar, most new entrants to this branch of the profession are graduates, though other possibilities exist (notably progression from a legal executive). The trainee is required to undertake a one-year vocational course organised by the Law Society. This is followed by a further two years' training (known as 'articles') with a qualified and experienced solicitor.

Newly-qualified solicitors will generally seek employment with an established practice as an assistant solicitor. They may then aspire to a partnership or establish their own practice. Alternatively, they may obtain employment in both the public and private sectors.

Legal executives

Legal executives perform professional work under the guidance of a solicitor. They tend to specialise in particular areas of the law. Their governing body is the Institute of Legal Executives. Once qualified, a legal executive is entitled to undertake the Law Society training programme and qualify as a solicitor.

The Crown Prosecution Service

Since 1985, a major new public sector employment opportunity for barristers and solicitors has been the Crown Prosecution Service (which also employs unqualified staff). The CPS was established by the Prosecution of Offences Act 1985 to take over the greater part of the police role in prosecutions. The police are still responsible for charging a person with an offence. Thereafter, the CPS is responsible for the conduct of the prosecution, including reviewing at all stages whether or not it should be continued (though it must still hire private barristers to conduct Crown Court prosecutions).

The Code for Crown Prosecutors (issued by the Director of Public Prosecutions under section 10 of the 1985 Act) creates a two-part test for the continuation of prosecutions:

(a) **evidential sufficiency:** there must be admissible, substantial and reliable evidence that the accused committed the offence. There must also be a realistic prospect of conviction, not merely a bare *prima facie* case.

(b) **public interest:** the prosecution must also be in the public interest. The Code specifies a number of relevant considerations:

(i) the likely penalty: the prosecutor must be satisfied that the likely penalty justifies the time and cost of proceedings.

(ii) staleness: the prosecutor should be cautious in proceeding if the last offence was committed more than three years prior to the likely date of trial.

(iii) youth: serious consideration should be given to the alternative of a caution (where appropriate) in cases involving young adults.

(iv) old age: except where the offence is a serious one, the prosecutor should be cautious in continuing proceedings against the elderly and infirm.

(v) mental illness: caution should be exercised in proceedings against the mentally ill, taking into account the likely effect of proceedings on the person's mental health.

(vi) sexual offences: the prosecutor should consider the age of each participant and whether there was an element of seduction or corruption.

(vii) the attitude of the complainant.

(viii) peripheral involvement: in general, proceedings should only be taken against those centrally involved in the offence.

If, having taken into account such of these considerations as are relevant, the prosecutor is still in doubt, he should consider the attitude of the local community and the prevalence of the offence. If still in doubt, the decision should be to prosecute.

There are special guidelines relating to the prosecution of juveniles. The prosecutor should consider the general issue of the juvenile's welfare, and there is a presumption in favour of alternatives to prosecution, where appropriate (for example, cautions).

An analysis of the present organisation of the profession

There are three main areas of concern regarding the present organisation of the legal profession:

Social composition: most entrants to the legal profession come from a middle class background. Both women and the ethnic minorities are significantly under-represented. It may be argued that this deters able people of alternative backgrounds from entering the profession and may also create a social distance between professional and client. This contributes to the inaccessibility of the profession both as career and service.

However, the profession itself has taken some measures to address these problems. The Law Society has programmes to encourage women and ethnic minorities and the Bar Council has established a number of scholarships. Also, the 1990 Act places barristers under the obligations of the Sex Discrimination Act 1975 and the Race Relations Act 1976 when allocating pupillage and tenancies.

Also, this situation is not unique to the legal profession. Where entry to higher education is still largely limited to the middle class, it is not surprising that this is reflected in an essentially graduate profession. Nevertheless, though the situation has improved in recent years, further long-term measures need to be taken to ensure the profession reflects more accurately the social, gender and ethnic composition of the society it serves.

Efficiency of a divided profession: the formal division of the profession has been a controversial issue for some years. Both the

Benson Commission (1979) and the Marre Committee (1988) argued for retaining the division. However, a significant body of opinion continues to argue for fusion into a single profession. While this may have some advantages (for example, some reduction in the cost of legal services), there are also potential disadvantages (such as a possible decline in the availability of specialists). Also, in those jurisdictions (for example, the USA) where there is no formal (or *de jure*) division, there still tends to be an informal (or *de facto*) distinction between office lawyers and trial lawyers. It would seem, therefore, that the fusion debate is inconclusive. Furthermore, the 1990 Act removed many of the distinctions between the two branches, notably regarding advocacy rights, and it will be some time before the consequences of this can be assessed.

Accountability: it is often argued that the profession is insufficiently accountable for the quality of the service it provides. A particular concern relates to the professional immunity in contract and tort for negligent advocacy (the 'advocate's immunity'). This extends to the conduct of a case in court (*Rondel v. Worsley* (1969)) and pre-trial work closely connected with it (*Saif Ali v. Sydney Mitchell & Co* (1980)). The immunity is justified as being in the public interest: the advocate has a duty to the court as well as to the client, and should not be deterred in the performance of this duty by the threat of litigation. However, it is difficult to see why lawyers should be more privileged than other professional groups (for example, doctors, accountants, architects), particularly when it is remembered that the issue is liability for negligence, not mere errors of judgment.

The dissatisfied client may also complain to the appropriate governing body. This self-regulation was strengthened by the 1990 Act, which established a Legal Services Ombudsman (which deals with complaints about the way in which the governing body has dealt with a complaint). Again, it remains to be seen how effective this new measure will be.

4. THE PROVISION OF LEGAL SERVICES

Introduction

The principle of the rule of law is at the heart of the English legal system. This states, among other things, that all citizens are equal before the law. However, for this notional equality to have any practical meaning, individuals must have access to the system and institutions that uphold this principle. Therefore, the question of equal access to legal services is a fundamental one if all citizens are to benefit from the law and its protections. However, this equality of access does not exist. Rather, there is what has been termed an *unmet need* for legal services. Research carried out in the 1970s by Abel-Smith, Zander and Brooke identified three forms of unmet need:

(a) where someone does not recognise their problem as a legal one;

(b) where the problem is recognised as legal, but the person is unable to access the services available to provide help;

(c) where the problem is recognised as legal, but no developed service exists to provide the appropriate help.

The reasons for the unmet need

P. Harris (*Introduction to Law*, 4th ed., Butterworths) identifies four main factors (or barriers to access) which create the unmet need:

The geographical factor: lawyers tend to be located in areas convenient to their traditional client-base (the property owning and commercial classes). This has led to an imbalance in the distribution of legal services, both locally and nationally. Locally, lawyers tend to be based in the business area of town, rather than in industrial or residential areas. This can make it difficult for the non-propertied classes to access their services. It will often require taking time off work and additional expense, over and above the cost of the lawyer's services. Nationally, the Benson Commission on Legal Services (1979) found that there were far more lawyers per head of population in the commercial and light industrial south of the country than in the heavy industrial north. This did not mean that people in the northern communities had less need of legal services. Rather, it meant that the profession was more concerned with providing for the needs of prosperous, home-owning business communities than for those of urban, working-class, industrial communities.

The psychological factor: the essentially middle class nature of the profession frequently creates a social distance between lawyer and non-propertied client. This makes the law seem to many to be an alien and intimidating world, and one with which they are reluctant to become involved.

The knowledge factor: relatively few lawyers will have a detailed knowledge of areas of law which are not directly relevant to the needs of their traditional clients. Therefore, they are frequently ill-equipped to meet the needs of non-propertied clients.

The cost factor: many people simply cannot afford the cost of private legal services. Civil litigation, for example, involves costs of many thousands of pounds. This is a financial risk that is clearly beyond the means of many people and a considerable deterrent to many more.

It may be argued, therefore, that the legal profession has systematically failed to provide a range of services which are appropriate and affordable for all sections of society, preferring to concentrate on the needs of the propertied and commercial classes.

Resolving the unmet need

There are three main strategies available for resolving the unmet need for legal services:

(a) the use of public funds to subsidise the cost of private legal services (the subsidy solution).

The use of subsidies has been the main way in which attempts have been made to resolve the unmet need. State funding of legal services was introduced by the Legal Aid and Advice Act 1949. This was intended to provide for the unmet need in three ways:

   (a) by subsidising the cost of litigation and representation (legal aid)

(b) by subsidising the cost of preliminary and non-contentious work (legal advice and assistance)

(c) by establishing a national network of public solicitors.

The plan for a public solicitor service was never implemented. The two remaining elements require further discussion:

Legal advice and assistance: public funding for legal advice and assistance was not in fact introduced until the Legal Advice and Assistance Act 1972 established the 'Green Form' scheme. This allows solicitors to perform a small amount of cash-limited work for those who qualify under a means test. This work includes the giving of advice, writing letters and drafting documents. The Legal Aid Act 1979 extended the scheme to include limited forms of representation (for example, before the Mental Health Review Tribunal and in domestic proceedings at the magistrates' court). This is known as Assistance By Way Of Representation (ABWOR). A person facing possible criminal proceedings may also receive preliminary advice and assistance though the duty solicitor schemes that operate at police stations and magistrates' courts.

Civil legal aid: to qualify for legal aid for civil litigation and representation, the applicant must satisfy both a means and merits test The scheme is administered by an independent Legal Aid Board (with regional and local committees). The means test involves an assessment of the applicant's disposable income and capital. If this is below a certain level, full aid may be available. If above a certain level, no aid will be available. If between these two levels, some aid may be available, with the applicant being required to make a graduated contribution to their own costs. The merits test requires the applicant to show that he has reasonable grounds for taking, defending or being a party to the proceedings in question.

Criminal legal aid: again, the applicant must satisfy both a means and merits test. The means test is similar to that for civil legal aid. The merits test, administered by the clerk to the court, requires the granting of aid to be desirable in the interests of justice. This is decided by the application of the 'Widgery criteria' (established in 1966 by the Widgery Committee on Legal Aid in Criminal Proceedings, and later incorporated into the Legal Aid

Act 1988). For example, aid is desirable where the charge is so grave that the applicant is at serious risk of losing his liberty; or where the granting of aid is desirable in the interests of someone other than the accused (for example, in sexual offences, where it is undesirable that the victim be cross-examined by the alleged perpetrator).

Evaluation: the legal aid system is subject to a number of criticisms:

(a) it only tackles one of the barriers to access, that of cost. Any strategy that only addresses part of the problem can only ever be part of the solution.

(b) it is not cost-effective. The state faces a dilemma between ever-increasing costs and cutbacks in the level of provision. In fact, while costs have steadily risen (to over £1 billion per year), the proportion of the population eligible for aid has fallen from approximately two-thirds in 1979 to around one-third in 1991.

(c) this has resulted in what is known as the 'middle income trap', where a significant proportion of the population are not eligible for legal aid but cannot afford to pay for legal services themselves.

(d) some claim that legally-aided clients receive a second class service compared to that offered to private, fee-paying clients.

(e) with the growth in use of alternative mechanisms to the courts (such as tribunals), concerns have been expressed that legal aid is rarely available in these circumstances.

(f) with regard to criminal legal aid, there are concerns over inconsistencies in the application of the Widgery criteria in magistrates' courts. This raises the danger that some people may be convicted because they are not adequately represented.

Therefore, it seems that the present reliance on the use of subsidies is unlikely to resolve the unmet need for legal services.

(b) encouraging the profession to diversify into neglected areas of provision (the diversification solution).

The profession has itself taken some measures to increase accessibility and tackle the unmet need. The Law Society has introduced initiatives such as the £5 fixed-fee interview scheme and the Accident Liability Advice Scheme to offer low cost or free preliminary advice. The Bar Council funds the Free Representation Unit, where barristers will take up public interest cases free of charge. However, such schemes are only likely to have a very small impact on the level of unmet need. The economics of private sector legal services mean that the profession will inevitably continue to concentrate on the needs of the propertied and commercial classes.

(c) establishing alternative and complementary forms of provision (the complementary solution).

There is a wide range of alternative sources of legal advice:

   (a) local authority advice units (typically covering housing, benefit and consumer issues)
   (b) charities
   (c) trade unions
   (d) the motoring organisations
   (e) the broadcast and print media
   (f) private insurance schemes.
However, the major contribution in this area comes from two sources:

Citizens Advice Bureaux: there are approximately 700 CABx throughout Britain. They deal with approximately 7 million enquiries per year, of which it is estimated that around one-third involve legal issues. Given their geographical distribution, informal atmosphere, specialist knowledge of issues such as welfare, housing, immigration, and so on, and the fact that their advice is free, the CABx seem to address all the factors giving rise to the unmet need, and would appear to have a key role to play in any successful strategy to resolve it. The Benson Commission viewed the CABx as excellently placed to provide a preliminary advice and referral service. However, they would require a significant increase in funding to perform this role effectively.

Law Centres: there are approximately 60 law centres, located in London and the other major metropolitan areas. They share the advantages of CABx outlined above, with the additional benefit of being specifically concerned with legal issues. Their work was similarly praised by the Benson Commission, and could make a major impact, together with CABx, in a coordinated approach to addressing the unmet need. However, inadequate and insecure funding limits their ability to do so.

Access to Justice Act 1999

5. LAY PARTICIPATION IN THE ADMINISTRATION OF JUSTICE

Introduction

One of the more remarkable features of the English legal system is the extent to which lay persons are involved in the administration of justice, particularly the criminal justice system. Some lay persons are brought into the system for their particular expertise (for example, tribunal members, lay assessors in the Admiralty Court). However, the principal justification for the two main lay institutions, the magistracy and the jury, is their *amateur* nature. This ensures that the values and common sense of the non-professional have a role to play in the system. Both these institutions have a long history: the first magistrates (also known as Justices of the Peace) were appointed in 1195 and assumed a judicial role in the fourteenth century; the importance of the jury in deciding criminal trials dates from 1215 and the decision of the Fourth Lateran Council to withdraw Church support for trial by ordeal. By 1367 it was established that the jury's verdict had to be unanimous, and in Bushell's Case (1670) it was established that the jury had the right to bring in a verdict according to its conscience.

Magistrates

There are over 30,000 lay magistrates in England and Wales. While they do have some civil jurisdiction (for example, in family and licensing matters), their main responsibilities concern the criminal law. Approximately 95 per cent of all criminal trials take place in the magistrates' court. The role of the magistrate is, therefore, an important and prominent one.

Lay magistrates are part-time, amateur judges. They are unpaid, though they do receive allowances for travel, subsistence and loss of earnings. No formal qualifications are required to be a magistrate, though some people (such as undischarged bankrupts) are disqualified from serving.

Magistrates are appointed by the Lord Chancellor following a recommendation from a Local Advisory Committee. The committee must have one representative from each of the major political parties. However, most members are either serving or retired magistrates. Vacancies for new magistrates are sometimes advertised in the local press. Volunteers are also sought from local political parties and community groups. The majority of appointments, however, are made from those known personally or by reputation to members of the committee.

While lay magistrates are amateur justices, they have, since 1966, received some formal training in their duties. The initial training concentrates on jurisdiction, procedure and sentencing. Thereafter, refresher training continues the emphasis on sentencing exercises and also deals with any relevant new legislation.

The lay magistracy has been subject to a number of criticisms:

Social composition: it is argued that the Advisory Committee system, together with financial and employment constraints, produces a magistracy that is predominantly white and middle class. Approximately 80 per cent of magistrates are from the professional and managerial classes. This clearly contradicts the aim of a magistracy that it is representative of the local community.

Inadequate training: it is sometimes argued that magistrates receive insufficient training. The limited nature of their training is based on three arguments: firstly, that magistrates are appointed for their *existing* qualities of judgement and responsibility; secondly, that new magistrates learn their role by sitting alongside experienced colleagues; thirdly, that expert legal advice is available from the clerk to the court. This does, however, raise the danger that magistrates can become too reliant on the clerk.

Prosecution and conviction mindedness: it is argued that many magistrates are, by virtue of their social background, too ready to side with the prosecution and the police.

Inconsistencies in sentencing: studies have shown considerable inconsistencies in sentencing from one Bench to another. However, some degree of inconsistency is inevitable if magistrates are to reflect local concerns.

However, alternatives to the lay magistracy, such as an increased use of full-time, paid magistrates (known as stipendiaries), would be far more expensive than the present system. Also, and most significantly, it would remove an important element of community involvement in the criminal justice system. Nevertheless, if the lay magistracy is to continue, steps must be taken to reform the appointments process to ensure that its social, racial and gender composition more accurately reflects that of the local community it serves. This is essential to maintain public confidence in the magistracy.

Juries

The use of the jury in civil cases is now rare, being largely confined to actions for false imprisonment and defamation (where juries have been criticised for awarding excessively high levels of compensation). The following discussion, therefore, will focus on the use of juries in serious criminal trials at the Crown Court.

A criminal jury consists of twelve members and it is their role to decide questions of fact and reach a verdict. They receive no training, though there has been a recent pilot scheme where jurors have been shown a short explanatory video.

The qualifications for jury service are laid down in the Juries Act 1974. Any person who is aged between 18 and 70, is on the electoral register, and has been a resident of the United Kingdom for at least five years is eligible for jury service. However, some people are or may be excluded:

Ineligible for service: some people, such as members of the clergy or religious orders and the mentally ill, are ineligible.

Disqualified from service: others, such as those with a significant criminal record, are disqualified.

Excusal as of right: others, such as doctors and nurses, those with previous jury service, and those over 65 years of age, have a right to be excused service should they request this.

Excusal for good cause: any person may request to be excused jury service for good cause. This includes situations where service would cause personal hardship: for example, pregnant women.

If a juror becomes indisposed during the trial, the case will continue unless the number of jurors remaining falls below nine. The jury must attempt to reach an unanimous verdict. However, where following a minimum of two hours' deliberation, they are unable to do so, the judge may accept a majority verdict. With a jury of twelve or eleven members, at least ten must agree; with ten members, nine must agree; with the minimum of nine members, the verdict must be unanimous. If the jury falls below the minimum number or fails to reach a verdict, the case is discharged and may be re-tried before another jury.

It is difficult to research the workings of the jury, as the Contempt of Court Act 1981 prohibits the questioning of jurors. However, studies of 'shadow' juries reveal that while jurors generally take their role seriously, there is no standard pattern to their deliberations and the panel can be dominated by one or two strong-minded individuals.

The main arguments for the continued use of the jury are:

The symbolic value of community participation in the most serious criminal trials: it is thought to be important that questions of this sort are decided by ordinary members of society, not by a legal elite.

The 'perverse' verdict: the right of the jury to bring in a verdict according to its conscience is one of the few ways in which ordinary citizens can comment directly upon the merits of a particular law or prosecution.

However, there have been criticisms made of the jury system:

The jury is open to intimidation: this possibility has led to the removal of jury trial in Northern Ireland for terrorist offences, which are tried before a judge alone in a so-called 'Diplock' court.

Jurors cannot understand complex evidence: this has been a particular concern regarding fraud cases. In 1986 the Roskill Committee recommended replacing the jury in such cases with two expert lay assessors, though this has not been implemented. Some commentators have also called for a raising of the lower age limit for jury service and for the introduction of some form of comprehension test.

As with the magistracy, any alternative to the jury, such as a panel of judges, would tend to increase costs and remove the element of community participation. Again, therefore, there would seem to be no viable alternative to the continued use of the jury.

6. THE JUDICIARY

Introduction

The judge performs a number of important functions:
  (a) the judge supervises the conduct of the trial;
  (b) the judge decides any questions of law that arise during the trial;
  (c) in most civil cases, the judge also decides questions of fact, reaches a verdict and awards a remedy;
  (d) in criminal trials, the judge sums up the evidence to the jury and directs them as to the law they must apply in reaching their verdict. Following conviction, it is the judge who passes sentence;
  (e) in performing the above, the judge must interpret and apply both statute and common law. This is a particularly important aspect of the work of the judges in the superior courts.
Given this central role, both in the administration of justice and the development of the law, three issues relating to the judiciary assume great importance:

(a) judicial appointments and training

Most judicial appointees are barristers and, although the Courts and Legal Services Act 1990 increased the potential for solicitor-judges, this is likely to remain the case for the foreseeable future.

Appointments (apart from the senior judicial offices) are made by the Lord Chancellor. For the junior judicial posts (of Assistant Recorder, Recorder and Circuit Judge), applications are invited. For the senior judicial posts (of High Court (or puisne) Judge, Lord Justice of Appeal and Lord of Appeal in Ordinary (Law Lord)), appointment is by invitation, not application.

The five senior judicial offices are:

(a) *The Lord Chancellor.* This is a political appointment, made by the monarch on the advice of the Prime Minister. The Lord Chancellor is a senior member of the government, whose department is responsible for most aspects of the administration of justice (though some aspects fall under the Home Office). Therefore, the Lord Chancellor is a member of the Executive, the Judiciary and the Legislature (as a member of the House of Lords). This is a very peculiar constitutional position and clearly at odds with the theory of the separation of powers. This has led some to argue that the Lord Chancellor's executive functions should be taken away and given to a new Minister of Justice. While this proposal has some merit in terms of efficiency and accountability, it is unlikely to be adopted in the foreseeable future.

(b) *the Lord Chief Justice.* This is the senior full-time judicial appointment. The Lord Chief Justice presides over the Court of Appeal (Criminal Division) and the Queen's Bench Division of the High Court.

(c) *The Master of the Rolls*, who presides over the Court of Appeal (Civil Division).

(d) *the Vice-Chancellor*, who is the effective head of the Chancery Division of the High Court.

(e) *the President of the Family Division of the High Court.*

Judges hold office 'during good behaviour'. They can only be dismissed for a breach of this obligation or by an address in both Houses of Parliament. Otherwise, a judge will remain in office until he either resigns or reaches the retirement age of 70.

New judicial appointees receive little formal training. Since 1979, this training has been administered by the Judicial Studies Board. At present, the training consists of a one-week residential course

following appointment (with an emphasis on procedure and
sentencing). This is followed by at least one week sitting alongside
an experienced judge. Thereafter, the judge will attend occasional
refresher courses and seminars.

Evaluation: four main criticisms have been made of the present
approach to judicial appointments and training:
   (a) the appointments process is too informal and secret. There
       is considerable support for the establishment of an inde-
       pendent Judicial Appointments Commission (with both pro-
       fessional and lay representation) to oversee a more formal
       and open process. It is argued that this is necessary to
       broaden the social, racial and gender composition of the
       judiciary. Other possible reforms, such as the election of
       judges or parliamentary confirmation of senior appoint-
       ments have received little support, largely because of the
       risk of compromising the independence of the judiciary.
       Nevertheless, while it is unclear as to the extent to which
       this social exclusivity damages judicial performance or
       public confidence, it does seem desirable that the social,
       ethnic and gender composition of the judiciary should more
       accurately reflect that of the society it serves.
   (b) the age of the judiciary. Most judges are appointed in their
       early 50s and the retirement age is 70. Concerns have been
       expressed that this contributes to judicial remoteness. How-
       ever, the only way of appointing younger judges would be to
       establish a career judiciary (such as that in France), where
       younger lawyers could elect to undertake further training
       for a judicial career.
   (c) judicial performance has been subject to increasing media
       criticism. Judges do, from time to time, make observations
       and pass sentences which seem to be out of step with public
       opinion. While such instances are rare, and the appeal pro-
       cess exists to correct any mistakes or unfairness that results,
       it is possible that this does damage public confidence in the
       judiciary. However, it must be remembered that media criti-
       cisms are not always well-founded, with judges often being
       blamed for defects in the law over which they have no
       control.
   (d) the training programme is inadequate. Again, this could
       probably ony be remedied with the establishment of a career
       judiciary.

(b) judicial independence

The independence of the judiciary is a necessary condition of impartiality and, therefore, of a fair trial. This means that judges should be free from pressure by the Executive, particular interest groups and litigants.

Formal independence is guaranteed in a number of ways:
  (a) judicial salaries and pensions are determined by an independent review body.
  (b) judges should not hold any other paid appointment or carry on any other profession or business while in office.
  (c) judges should disqualify themselves from any case where they might (or might appear to) be biased or in which they have a personal interest. This emphasises the importance of appearances: not only must justice be done, it must be seen to be done.
  (d) a judge cannot be sued for acts either done within jurisdiction or for which he honestly believed at the time to be within jurisdiction (*Sirros v. Moore* (1975)). This immunity rests on the public interest justification that the judge should not be deterred in the performance of his duties by the threat of litigation.

The informal independence of the judiciary from the other branches of the state is less certain. This independence is essential if the judiciary is to act as an effective check on the Executive via judicial review. Some (such as Griffith) have argued that judges cannot, because of their background and position, be politically neutral and tend to be conservative in outlook. Others (such as Lord Denning) argue that the judges are perfectly capable of providing an effective check on government. While recent evidence would seem to support the latter view, it is doubts over this informal independence which lead some to fear any extension of judicial influence under a Bill of Rights.

(c) the judge as law-maker

Judges are involved in the law-making process in a number of ways:
  (a) through their participation in various advisory committees, commissions and inquiries;
  (b) through the participation of the Law Lords in the legislative

business of the House of Lords, though this is limited by
convention to law reform measures and issues of legal
technicality;

(c) through their role as the definitive interpreters of
legislation;

(d) through their responsibility for the development and evolution of the common law and Equity.

For many years the judiciary denied that they had any law-making
role, arguing that they merely declared the law as laid down by
statute or the fundamental principles of common law. However, in
recent times the judiciary has increasingly abandoned the fiction
of this declaratory approach and acknowleded that they do exercise
a law-making role.

Lee argues that there are three main factors which influence
judicial law-making:

(a) the previous history of legislative development;

(b) the consequences of the present law and the likely consequences of any given change;

(c) the judiciary's own perception of the proper limits of their
law-making role.

Given this variety of influences, it is not surprising that differences
can be observed in judicial approach. Harris contrasts two judicial
'styles':

(a) the *Formal Style*, characterised by caution and a tendency to
rely on formal devices such as distinguishing;

(b) the *Grand Style*, characterised by boldness and a wilingness
to recognise issues of policy as well as principle.

Paterson observed similar variations in judicial approaches to
'hard' cases:

(a) the positive response (similar to the Grand Style);

(b) the adaptive response (similar to the Formal Style);

(c) to withdraw on the basis that the proposed change is
properly one for Parliament to make.

It is this last point, regarding the proper relationship between
courts and Parliament in the law-making process, that seems to
highlight the differences in judicial approach. One judge to have
written on this relationship was Lord Devlin. He drew a distinction
between:

(a) activist law-making by which he meant changing and developing the law *in response* to changes in the social consensus.

(b) dynamic law-making by which he meant changing and developing the law *in order to promote* change in the social
consensus.

For Lord Devlin, while it was proper for judges to engage in activist law-making, dynamic law-making should be left to Parliament. He also pointed out that judges had far less scope and authority for law-making when dealing with statute than when dealing with the common law.

Therefore, while allowing for variations in judicial approach, it seems clear that there are three main constraints on judicial law-making:

(a) the judge is bound by the rules of precedent when dealing with the common law;

(b) the judge is bound by the rules of statutory interpretation when dealing with statutes;

(c) the judge is bound by his own perception of the proper limits of the judiciary's law-making role and of the superior role of Parliament in the law-making partnership with the courts.

Defined and limited in this way, judicial law-making is an important and beneficial aspect of the law-making process in a common law system. There are, however, a number of reforms which could be introduced to enhance the effectiveness of this role:

(a) a formal procedure by which the courts could refer issues to Parliament where it is felt that further development is beyond the scope of legitimate judicial lawmaking;

(b) the introduction of an independent advisor in the appellate courts to perform a similar role to that of the Advocate General in the Court of Justice of the European Union;

(c) the provision of research attorneys to the judiciary in the appellate courts. This role could form an important element in the training of a career judiciary.

Section Three: THE IDEA OF LAW

1. LEGAL PERSONALITY

Introduction

The term 'legal personality' is used to indicate those individuals and organisations that the law recognises as having their own, independent, legal existence. It is an important concept, because it is the precise nature of someone's legal personality that defines their legal rights, duties and status. There are two basic forms of legal personality:

(a) **natural legal personality:** all human beings have their own legal personality;

(b) **juristic (or artificial) legal personality:** some organisations have their own legal personality, separate from the individuals who form that organisation.

Natural legal personality

While all human beings have natural legal personality, they do not all share the same type of personality. The law has to discriminate between different types of people in order to identify their particular rights and duties, to grant them a particular status. For example, the law discriminates between employer and employee, landlord and tenant, trader and consumer, British citizen, E.U. citizen and foreign national. This form of discrimination is clearly inevitable and acceptable. Sometimes it is done to protect certain groups of people from exploitation. For example, in the civil law, particular rules apply regarding the contractual capacity of minors and the mentally incapacitated. Similarly, special provision is made regarding the criminal liability of children and the mentally disordered. In other cases it is done to take account of practical realities. For example, members of the armed services or merchant navy are not, while on active service, subject to the normal legal formalities when making a will.

However, not all forms of discrimination, for example on grounds of race or sex, are justifiable or desirable. Here, the law has been used in an attempt to enforce *equality* of treatment. It must be remembered, however, that establishing formal legal equality of rights is only one aspect (albeit an important and symbolic one) of a general strategy to eliminate this sort of undesirable discrimination. Also, there are some aspects of natural legal personality which remain problematic and controversial, due to the law's failure to adapt to social or technological change: the rights and status of the unborn child, the medical management of death, and the position of transsexuals being prominent examples. However, many of these areas involve issues of social controversy, and it would be harsh to blame the law for failing to resolve its responses to issues which fiercely divide society itself.

Juristic (or artificial) legal personality

The law grants a separate legal personality to certain forms of organisation; those which have been *incorporated*. There are two basic types of corporation:

(a) **the corporation sole:** this refers to certain offices of unlimited duration, such as the Crown and some clerical offices. The main reason for giving the office its own legal identity is to ensure the legal continuity of the office and its activities, regardless of changes in the individual office-holder.

(b) **the corporation aggregate:** this refers to incorporated organisations of more than one person. This type of corporation can be created in three ways:
   (i) by Royal Charter (for example, the BBC)

(ii) by Act of Parliament (for example, further education corporations)

(iii) under the Companies Acts

This last category requires further explanation. Companies are generally organisations of limited liability. This means that the liability of individual shareholders is limited to the value of shares owned. Because it has its own legal identity, the debts of the company remain the debts of the company, not the shareholders. This is in clear contrast with (and an advantage over) unincorporated organisations, such as partnerships. Here, because the organisation has no separate legal personality, the individual members remain fully liable for the debts of the firm.

The company may be either a private limited company (given the designation 'Ltd') or, where there is an open market in its shares, a public limited company (given the designation 'plc'). The main reasons for the development of the limited liability company were economic. As it both limits investment risk and enables efficient commercial practices, the limited liability company has been essential to industrial and economic development from the nineteenth century onwards.

As far as its civil legal identity is concerned (the ability to enter contracts, sue and be sued, own property and so on), the development of corporate personality has been largely successful. However, the issues surrounding corporate criminal liability, where company policy or actions result in the commission of a crime, have been less successfully addressed. With the exception of strict liability offences, the prosecution must establish corporate *mens rea* by showing that a natural person within the corporation, and who can be taken to represent its controlling or directing mind (for example, the managing director), had the required *mens rea* for the offence concerned. This often proves to be an extremely difficult task.

2. LAW AND MORALITY

Introduction

Both law and morality are concerned with the regulation of social conduct. Therefore, they share many similar, though not synonymous, features:

Moral Codes	Legal Codes
General statements of principle.	Precise rules or norms of behaviour.
Voluntary subscription.	Compulsory subscription.
Informal enforcement (through, for example, peer group pressure).	Formal enforcement (through, for example, the police and the courts).
Concerned with how people *ought* to behave.	Concerned with how people *shall* behave.

It is this contrast between 'ought' and 'shall', highlighting concerns over whether the law should be used to enforce particular moral values, which has proved the most problematic aspect of the relationship between law and morality.

The relationship between law and morality exists for both historical and functional reasons:

Historically: legal codes tend to emerge from moral codes. In primitive societies, there is often little or no difference between the two. However, as a society grows larger and more sophisticated, this close relationship begins to fracture. As the society becomes more diverse (socially, culturally, economically and morally), the need for a distinct and universally applicable set of rules (a legal system) emerges. Thus, while links between the legal and moral codes remain, these tend to become increasingly insecure and sometimes controversial.

Functionally: both law and morality are used to perform similar social tasks, in that they are both employed to preserve order and maintain acceptable standards of behaviour through the promotion and enforcement of rules and principles.

Thus, it is not surprising that the relationship between law and morality is a complex one, and that moral influences pervade much of the law. However, this is not to suggest that all that may be regarded as immoral is necessarily illegal (for example, adultery) or *vice versa* (for example, parking offences).

The moral influence in English law

Moral notions form the background or context of many aspects of English law, with its concerns for the protection of the person, property, the family and so on. This reflects the influence of an essentially Judaeo-Christian moral tradition. However, as noted above, the legal rules will tend to be more specific and precise than their moral counterparts. For example, while there may be a general moral precept against telling lies, this will only be illegal in certain specific circumstances (such as perjury and fraud). In the vast majority of instances, this moral context or background is uncontroversial. Indeed, it may be seen as beneficial, as it tends to enhance the legitimacy of the law and encourage the observance of legal rules.

However, problems may arise where moral issues become foregrounded, rather than merely providing a background context, *i.e.* where the law is used specifically to enforce particular moral positions. In the legislative sphere, this can be seen in the Abortion Act 1967 and the Obscene Publications Act 1956 (with its problematic test of a tendency to deprave and corrupt). Similarly, in the judicial sphere, this is evident in the common law offences of conspiracy to corrupt public morals (*Shaw v. DPP* (1962); *Knuller (Publishing, Printing and Promotions) Ltd v. DPP* (1973)) and conspiracy to outrage public decency (*R v. Gibson* (1991)). Moral values can also be seen to have exercised a clear, though indirect, influence in a range of other cases; for example, those relating to sexual conduct (*R v. Brown and others* (1993)). The legal foregrounding of a particular moral position becomes problematic where the social consensus on that issue has broken down or fragmented and, as indicated above, the more diverse a society becomes, the greater the potential for such fragmentation.

In such circumstances, the law cannot simply withdraw from the issue unless and until consensus is restored: there cannot be any 'no-go' areas. The law must, therefore, identify an acceptable approach to issues of moral controversy. Three suggested approaches are:

(a) **the libertarian approach:** some writers, such as Schur and Hart, have argued that the law should not interfere in private behaviour except in order to prevent harm to others. However, it is sometimes difficult to identify the boundaries between private and public conduct and the limits of harm; for example, drug use may be a 'private' activity but can have 'public' and 'harmful' consequences, such as additional burdens on the public health system and criminal activity to 'feed the habit'. Furthermore, it is arguable that the consent of the participants does not necessarily make an activity 'victimless', and that there may be circumstances where it is justifiable to use the law to override individual consent.

(b) **the liberal approach:** this is typified in the approach adopted by the Wolfenden Committee on Homosexual Offences and Prostitution, which reported in 1957. The view of the Committee was that the law should not interfere in private behaviour except where necessary to preserve public order and decency, to protect against the offensive and injurious, and to safeguard individuals (particularly the most vulnerable) against corruption and exploitation. However, difficulties arise with this approach due to the subjective nature of the criteria advanced.

(c) **the duty/aspiration approach:** this arguably more satisfactory approach was advanced by Lon Fuller. He distinguished between what he termed the morality of duty and the morality of aspiration. The morality of duty indicates that standard of behaviour which most people would be prepared to tolerate, *i.e.* the bare minimum level of acceptable conduct. The morality of aspiration indicates that standard of behaviour which it is felt most people should aspire or seek to live up to. Thus, Fuller is seeking to come to terms with the problematic distinction between 'ought' and 'shall' indicated earlier. Fuller's solution was that while the law may be employed to enforce the morality of duty, it cannot and should not be used to enforce the morality of aspiration, *i.e.* it is legitimate to use the law to prevent people behaving badly, but not legitimate to use it in an attempt to force people to behave virtuously. This approach was echoed by Lord Devlin, when he argued that 'the law is concerned with the minimum and not with the maximum' (Patrick Devlin, *The Enforcement of Morals*, OUP, p. 19). It may also be seen in the famous 'neighbour principle' advanced by Lord Atkin in *Donoghue v. Stevenson* (1932):

'The liability for negligence . . . is no doubt based upon a general public sentiment of moral wrongdoing for which the offender must pay. But acts or omissions which any moral code would censure cannot in a practical world be treated so as to give a right to every person injured by them to demand relief. In this way rules of law arise which limit the range of complainants and the extent of their remedy. The rule that you are to love your neighbour becomes in law: you must not injure your neighbour, and the lawyer's question: who is my neighbour? receives a restricted reply'.

3. LAW AND FREEDOMS

Introduction

When considering the nature and protection of freedoms under English law, it is important to understand from the outset that any discussion takes place in a context of civil liberties, *not* civil rights. This distinction between 'liberties' and 'rights' is not simply a matter of a choice of words, but has profound consequences for the nature of freedom in this country. To say that a person is at liberty to do something is fundamentally different from saying that a person has a right to do something. Freedom in English law has always been an essentially *residual* concept: one is free to do everything that is left over once the law has said what one cannot do.

This notion that one is free to do anything except that which is prohibited by law (with its implicit reference to the traditional figure of the 'free-born Englishman') is a superficially attractive one. However, its attractions become less clear when it is remembered that there are no legal constraints on the ability of a sovereign Parliament to enact further restrictions on even the most fundamental of freedoms.

Clearly, some restrictions on absolute freedom can be justified either to protect individual interests or the collective interest as represented by the state. Nevertheless, as Robertson observes, 'Liberty in Britain is a state of mind rather than a set of legal rules' (Geoffrey Robertson, *Freedom, the Individual and the Law*, 7th ed. Penguin, at p. xiii). Whether a 'state of mind' is adequate to protect the most fundamental freedoms, as a Britain which is becoming increasingly politically, socially, economically and ethnically diverse moves into the twenty-first century, is a question which is generating much debate. The present nature of freedoms and their protections, together with this debate as to whether a more formal set of guarantees is necessary, must now be considered in further detail.

Particular freedoms and protections

Freedom of the person: the right to individual liberty is one of the most fundamental of all freedoms. Therefore, any restriction must be clearly necessary and justified. The most obvious justification is the detention of persons suspected of committing crime, those awaiting trial, and those convicted. The powers of the state in each of these areas is regulated by statute: the Police and Criminal Evidence Act 1984; the Bail Act 1976; and the Criminal Justice Act 1991 (as amended). However, the issue of police powers has always provoked controversy; for example, regarding the extended powers of detention under prevention of terrorism legislation, and the restrictions on the right to silence introduced by the Criminal Justice and Public Order Act 1994. The rights of people in their relations with the police are protected by the ancient writ of *habeus corpus* (requiring detention to be justified to a court), the right to legal advice and the duty solicitor schemes, and the activities of the Police Complaints Authority. Furthermore, a number of civil actions may be used to remedy any unlawful infringement of personal freedom: assault; wrongful arrest; false imprisonment; and malicious prosecution.

Another justifiable restriction on personal liberty relates to the issue of mental health. Under the Mental Health Act 1983, a person suffering from a mental disorder can be detained against their will, *provided* two doctors certify that this is necessary to protect the individual himself or society at large. Specific protection is offered as the validity of any such detention (or its continuation) may be challenged before the Mental Health Review Tribunal.

Freedom of speech and expression: while freedom of speech is an essential democratic right, it is also one which is subject to significant restrictions. A general level of censorship is imposed by the Obscene Publications Act 1959 and the common law offences of corrupting public morals and outraging public decency. More specific powers to censor, regulate and certify exist under the Cinemas Act 1985, the Video Recordings Act 1984, and the Indecent Displays (Control) Act 1991. Television broadcasting is regulated by the Broadcasting Act 1990, the Broadcasting Complaints Commission and the Broadcasting Standards Council. Newspapers are, for the moment, subject to self-regulation by the Press Complaints Commission. This is an area which generates almost constant controversy.

The Official Secrets Act 1939 protects information sensitive to national security. However, the Act has been criticised on many occasions for being too widely drawn, and a number of prosecutions (for example, that of Clive Ponting in 1985) have proved controversial. There have been repeated calls for greater openness and freedom of information in govenment. However, the law has a difficult task here in balancing legitimate national security concerns with the equally legitimate need for a democratic government to be subject to public scrutiny.

Less controversial restrictions are imposed by the law of defamation, which is designed to protect an individual's reputation from untrue and damaging allegations. The balance between the general interest in free speech and the individual's interest in protecting his good name is maintained through the availability of various defences (for example, fair comment on a matter of public interest).

Freedom of assembly and association: the freedom for people to associate together (for example, in political parties, pressure groups or trade unions) and to assemble together (for example, to hold meetings, rallies or protest marches) are, again, essential democratic rights. However, this needs to be balanced against the need to maintain public order and to enable others to pursue their own lawful and legitimate activities. Therefore, there are restrictions on freedom of association under the Public Order Act 1936 (which outlaws quasi-military organisations and the wearing of uniforms or military insignia by political groups originally introduced to counter the rise of the fascist 'blackshirts' in the 1930s), and the prevention of terrorism legislation (which outlaws paramilitary groups). More controversially, the right of employees at GCHQ (the government communications headquarters in Cheltenham) to belong to a trade union was removed in the 1980s, on grounds of national security.

Regarding freedom of assembly, the Public Order Act 1986 grants the police, together with local authorities, the power to regulate protest marches, and also incorporates three specific public order offences: riot; violent disorder; and affray. Further restrictions were introduced, despite considerable public opposition, by the Criminal Justice and Public Order Act 1994 in relation to 'raves', 'travellers' and protests.

There are, therefore, wide-ranging and significant restrictions on even the most fundamental freedoms. However, many of these restrictions may be justified and are balanced by a number of important protections. Nevertheless, the extent of the present restrictions, together with the ability of Parliament to extend them further, even in the face of considerable opposition, indicates the fundamental weakness of the traditional residual approach.

The European Convention on Human Rights

An alternative, more formal approach to the protection of fundamental rights and freedoms (and one to which Britain subscribes)
is the European Convention. This came into force in 1953 and,
since 1966, Britain has accepted the right of individual petition to
the European Court of Human Rights. The rights protected by the
convention are:

Article 2 — the right to life
Article 3 — freedom from torture, inhuman or degrading treat-
ment or punishment
Article 4 — freedom from slavery and forced labour
Article 5 — freedom of the person
Article 6 — the right to a fair, public and independent trial
Article 7 — freedom from retrospective criminal laws
Article 8 — the right to respect for private and family life, home
and correspondence
Article 9 — freedom of thought, conscience and religion
Article 10 — freedom of expression
Article 11 — freedom of assembly and association
Article 12 — the right to marry and found a family
Article 13 — the right to an effective remedy before a national
authority for violation of any rights or freedoms
protected under the Convention
Article 14 — freedom from discrimination

The First Protocol to the Convention added:

Article 1 — the right to the enjoyment of private property
Article 2 — the right to education
Article 3 — the right to free elections by secret ballot

It should be noted, however, that these are *not* absolute rights or
freedoms, as the Convention allows for restrictions to protect
national security, public order, health or morals, and the rights and
freedoms of others. Nevertheless, there is an important distinction
here from the residual approach. The presumption is against

restrictions, and the validity of any restriction can be tested in the Court.

While Article 13 requires signatory states to provide an effective national remedy for breaches of the convention, this does *not* oblige them to incorporate the convention itself into national law. Britain (unlike, for example, Germany and Italy) has not done so and, therefore, the Convention cannot be relied on directly in an English court: as Lord Ackner observed in *R v Home Secretary,* ex parte *Brind* (1991), the Convention 'not having been incorporated into English law . . . cannot be a source of rights and obligations'. This has led some to argue for the incorporation of the Convention as part of a process of more formal protection for freedoms in Britain.

A Bill of Rights for the United Kingdom?

Arguments for: there are six main arguments for the enactment of a formal Bill of Rights:

(a) it would provide better protection than the present residual approach and would make the exercise of power by the state more accountable;

(b) it would bring Britain into line with the great majority of other democratic nations;

(c) it would be a flexible approach, allowing for the interpretation and reinterpretation of statements of fundamental principle to meet changing needs and times;

(d) it would have a significant educational and symbolic value;

(e) it would provide individuals with a much quicker remedy than is possible through the European Court of Human Rights;

(f) it would allow cases to be settled by the English courts, thereby avoiding the damage done to Britain's international reputation when it loses a case in the European Court.

Arguments against: there are four principal arguments against a Bill of Rights:

(a) it is an 'un-British' way of doing things. However, this is an essentially nineteenth century view, strongly influenced by the constitutional writing of Dicey. Prior to this, both Magna Carta (1215) and the Bill of Rights 1689 had established statements of general principle. Furthermore, Britain made extensive use of written constitutions in the process of decolonisation in the 1950s and 1960s, and is a signatory to both the Universal Declaration of Human Rights and the European Convention on Human Rights.

(b) freedoms are already well-protected, both by the common law and specific statutes (such as those concerning race and sex discrimination). Therefore, a Bill of Rights is unnecessary. However, this piecemeal approach lacks the educational and symbolic value of a Bill of Rights.

(c) the English judiciary is too establishment-minded to be effective guardians of a Bill of Rights and are not equipped to interpret statements of general principle. However, this seems to ignore the record and experience of the judiciary in the field of judicial review, and the fact that the Privy Council performs precisely this function on behalf of some Commonwealth states.

(d) a Bill of Rights would be too much of a straightjacket, preventing the state from taking necessary action in emergencies. However, it is quite possible, as the European Convention illustrates, to allow for exceptions in the interest of national security.

If a Bill of Rights approach were to be adopted, this could be done by simply incorporating the European Convention into English law. However, this would require some modification and up-dating. Therefore, it would be more satisfactory to develop a modern English constitutional settlement, based upon the European Convention.

The question also arises as to how and to what extent the provisions of a Bill of Rights would be entrenched against repeal or amendment. Mechanisms such as a special parliamentary majority or a referendum could be used. Alternatively, entrenchment against implied repeal could be achieved by using a clause similar to section 2(4) of the European Communities Act 1972.

Finally, regarding enforcement, responsibility could be given to the Queen's Bench Divisional Court, which currently deals wih judicial review. Alternatively, the task could be given to the Privy Council or a new form of 'supreme' court could be established.

4. LAW AND JUSTICE

Introduction

It seems an obvious thing to say that the primary aim of any legal system is to deliver justice. However, it is far from obvious what

this actually means, as the concept of 'justice' is extremely difficult
to define. Not only are there a number of different definitions of
justice, but also the question 'what is justice?' means different
things in different contexts—is a particular law just? is the legal
system just? does the combination of law and system produce a just
result?

Definitions of Justice

(a) **Aristotlean justice:** one of the earliest attempts to formu-
    late a theory of justice was that undertaken by Aristotle. He
    argued that the basis of justice is fairness, and that this takes
    two forms:
    (i) *distributive justice*: whereby the law is used to ensure that
        social benefits and burdens are fairly distributed through-
        out society.
    (ii) *corrective justice*: whereby the legal system acts to correct
        attempts by individuals to disturb this fair distribution.
        However, it may be argued that this simply replaces the
        question 'what is just?' by 'what is fair?'

(b) **Utilitarian theory:** the central principle of utilitarianism is
    that society should be organised in such a way as to achieve
    the greatest happiness for the greatest number. Thus, a law
    is just where it brings about a net gain in happiness to the
    majority, even if it also results in increased distress or unhap-
    piness to a minority. It is this willingness to trade-off the
    unhappiness of the minority against the happiness of the
    majority that liberal theory finds most objectionable in this
    approach.

(c) **Liberal (or natural rights) theory:** liberal theory, in con-
    trast with utilitarianism, tends to judge the justice of any form
    of social organisation by the extent to which it protects its
    minorities and most vulnerable groups. Therefore, liberal the-
    ories of justice tend to incorporate notions of natural rights:
    that there are certain basic rights (God-given or otherwise) to
    which all people are entitled. However, this approach has its
    own problems, not least in establishing agreement over the

content and extent of any list of 'natural' rights. For example, the right to vote is now regarded as an essential and universal right. However, for many years this right was subject to a property qualification, and it was not one to which women were entitled until this century. A recent attempt to identify a universal set of rights and principles was undertaken by John Rawls. Rawls' theory was based upon a hypothesis of what a group of individuals, placed in what he termed the 'original position', would agree upon. The original position exists behind a 'veil of ignorance', *i.e.* the individuals would not know of their individual talents and circumstances (they do not know whether they are rich or poor, young or old, male or female, able or disabled, and so on). Therefore, Rawls argues, rational self-interest would lead each individual to agree a set of basic rights and principles which they would find acceptable if it turned out that they were the least advantaged of the group. However, persuasive though this hypothesis may seem, it does not resolve the question of precisely what those rights and principles should be. In fact, it seems to lead back to Aristotle's question—what is fair?

(d) **Libertarian (or market-based) theory:** libertarian theory, such as that of Nozick, argues that intervention in the natural (or market) distribution of advantages (as required by the other theories) is an unjust interference with the rights of the individual. Libertarian analysis only permits very limited intervention to prevent unjust distribution through, for example, theft and fraud.

Therefore, it seems that the question of abstract justice is at least as much a political one as it is a philosophical one.

Justice and the English legal system

Whether a particular law is just is, as indicated above, essentially a political question. However, consideration must also be given to whether the system is just, and whether that system produces a just outcome. This involves consideration of both *formal* justice (regarding the system) and *substantive* justice (regarding outcomes):

Formal justice: this requires a system of independent tribunals for the administration of law and the resolution of disputes. The existence of the formal trial and appellate courts, together with the various forms of alternative dispute resolution, ensures the English legal system meets this requirement. Formal justice also requires that these institutions follow known and fair rules and procedures. Again, this requirement is met through the rules of due process and fair procedure, rules regarding the admissibility of evidence, limitation periods and so on. An important contribution is also made by the rules of natural justice; for example, *audi alterem partem* (both sides must be heard). Finally, it is important that any citizen with a grievance has access to these institutions. Here it may be argued that more needs to be done to ensure this access, particularly for the poorest and least-advantaged sections of society.

Substantive justice: the English legal system has a variety of mechanisms to ensure just outcomes. Regarding the common law, the principle of *stare decisis*, together with devices such as overruling and distinguishing, enables the courts to work towards both the just development of the common law itself and a just outcome in any given case. The courts may also turn to the principles of Equity where the strict application of common law rules would lead to injustice. Furthermore, where the courts are unable to resolve such issues, either because they are dealing with statute or because they have reached the limits of proper common law development, Parliament may act to remedy matters through legislation (as, for example, with the Law Reform (Frustrated Contracts) Act 1943). Indeed, it is this capacity to be self-correcting which is one of the most important aspects of the English legal system's capacity to ensure just outcomes.

Section Four: THE LAW OF CONTRACT

1. GENERAL PRINCIPLES OF CONTRACT LAW

Put simply, a contract is an agreement enforceable by law. However, while all contracts are agreements, not all agreements are contracts. Therefore, a contract must be a *particular type* of agreement, which can be identified by certain specific characteristics. These contractual characteristics are:

(a) Offer

      Agreement

(b) Acceptance

          Bargain

(c) Consideration

              Contract

(d) Intention

(e) Capacity

a. Formation of Contract

Offer

An offer is a proposition put by one person (the *offeror*) to another (the *offeree*), together with an indication that they are willing to be bound by the terms of the offer should the other person accept it.

The proposition can be made orally, in writing or by conduct, and can be made to a specific individual, a specific group or to the world at large.

For the proposition to be regarded as an offer it must be clear, precise and capable of acceptance as it stands (*Harvey v. Facey* (1893); *Gibson v. Manchester City Council* (1979)).

Invitations to treat: an invitation to treat is a proposition indicating a willingness to consider offers made by others or to enter into negotiations. Therefore, it is important to be able to distinguish between offers and invitations to treat, as while an offer is binding once accepted, an invitation to treat is not. However, this is not always an easy distinction to make, as some propositions which are commonly thought of as offers are, in legal terms, only invitations to treat. Two common forms of invitation to treat are:

(a) displays of goods for sale, either in-store (*Pharmaceutical Society of Great Britain v. Boots Cash Chemists (Southern) Ltd* (1952)) or in a shop window (*Fisher v. Bell* (1961)). Here, the shop is not offering to sell the goods but is inviting customers to make offers to buy.

(b) advertisements (*Partridge v. Crittenden* (1968)). Again, the general position is that the advertiser is not offering to sell but is inviting offers to buy. However, an advertisement *may* be regarded as an offer where it forms the basis of a unilateral contract (see below, p. 85).

Once an offer has been made it will either be accepted or terminated. No offer remains open indefinitely.

Termination of offer

There are five ways in which an offer may be terminated:

(a) **Revocation:** an offer may be revoked (withdrawn) *at any time* prior to acceptance, even where the offer is stated to be open for a certain period of time (*Payne v. Cave* (1789)). A promise to keep the offer open for a certain period is not binding unless it is supported by consideration, *i.e.* it is an option purchased under a separate contract (*Routledge v. Grant* (1828)). For revocation to be effective, it must be *communicated* to the offeree. It should be noted that the 'postal rule' (see below, p. 82) does *not* apply to letters of revocation (*Byrne & Co v. Leon Van Tienhoven & Co* (1880)). However, communication does not have to be made by the offeror himself: communication via a reliable third party is effective (*Dickinson v. Dodds* (1876)).

(b) **Rejection:** rejection by the offeree immediately terminates the offer (*Hyde v. Wrench* (1840)). This includes not only straightforward refusals, but also *counter offers*. These are responses which seek to vary or amend the original offer and, therefore, reject it and establish a new offer in its place. However, it is important to distinguish counter offers from mere enquiries or requests for further information (for example, whether payment on credit terms is available). These sorts of enquiries do *not* terminate the offer (*Stevenson, Jacques & Co v. McLean* (1880)).

(c) **Lapse of time:** where the offer is stated to be open for a certain period of time, it will lapse once that time has expired. Where no time limit for acceptance is specified, the offer will lapse after a reasonable time (*Ramsgate Victoria Hotel Co v. Montefiore* (1866)).

(d) **Failure of condition:** where the offer is made subject to a condition, then it will lapse if that condition is not fulfilled (*Financings Ltd v. Stimson* (1962)).

(e) **Death of one of the parties:** death of the offeree terminates the offer. Death of the offeror will terminate the offer where the offeree has notice of the death prior to acceptance (*Re Whelan* (1897)). However, where the offeree is unaware of the death, the offer will only be terminated where the contract could not be fulfilled by the offeror's personal representatives (for example, where it is one for personal services) (*Bradbury v. Morgan* (1862)).

Acceptance

The general rule regarding acceptance is that it must *exactly match* the terms of the offer. As has been seen (see 'rejection' above), a response which seeks to vary or amend the terms of the offer is a counter-offer, not an acceptance.

Generally, for acceptance to be effective it must be communicated to the offeror, *i.e.* actually brought to his attention (*Entores Ltd v. Miles Far East Corporation* (1955)). Where the offer specifies a particular method of communication, acceptance is only effective if this method is used. Where the offer indicates a preferred (but not compulsory) method, then communication by any method which is at least as advantageous to the offeror will be effective (*Tinn v. Hoffman & Co* (1873); *Manchester Diocesan Council for Education v. Commercial and General Investments Ltd* (1969)).

The postal rule: the postal rule is the one significant exception to this general rule regarding communication of acceptance. Acceptance by post is effective (and therefore binding) as soon as it is posted (*Adams v. Lindsell* (1818)), even where the letter is delayed or lost in the post(*Household Fire and Carriage Accident Insurance Co v. Grant* (1879)), *provided* it was capable of delivery (*i.e.* correctly addressed and stamped) (*Re London and Northern Bank, ex parte Jones* (1900)).

However, the rule will only apply where:

(a) postal acceptance is specified by the offeror; or
(b) postal communication is reasonable in the circumstances.

Furthermore, the offeror can exclude the rule by stating in the offer that postal acceptance will only be effective upon receipt (*Holwell Securities Ltd v. Hughes* (1974)).

The postal rule also applies to analogous forms of non-instantaneous communication (such as cables and inland telemessages), but not to written communication transmitted instantaneously (such as telex and fax) (*Brinkibon Ltd v. Stahag Stahl GmbH* (1983)). This emphasises that it is the delay between despatch and receipt which is relevant, not the written nature of the communication.

Uncertainty

There may be rare cases where the parties believe they have reached agreement but the courts will decide that it is too vague or uncertain to be enforced (*Scammell G and Nephew Ltd v. Ouston* (1941)). However, the courts will attempt to remove any apparent uncertainty by reference to any previous dealings between the parties and to any relevant commercial custom and practice (*Hillas & Co Ltd v. Arcos Ltd* (1932)).

Consideration

As noted above, an agreement must be supported by consideration if it is to be a contract. Consideration is the element which transforms the agreement into a *bargain*. It is what one person does (executed consideration) or promises to do (executory consideration) in return for the act or promise of the other.

There are four main rules regarding consideration:

(a) it must be either a detriment to the promisee or a benefit to the promisor (though commonly it will be both), incurred by the promisee at the request of the promisor.

For example, A agrees to sell his car to B for £1000. A's consideration for B's promise to pay the £1000 is his promise to transfer ownership of the car. This is a detriment to A (he no longer owns the car) and also a benefit to B (who now owns the car).

(b) consideration must move from the promisee but need not move to the promisor (*Tweddle v. Atkinson* (1861)).

For example, A's promise to give C £100 is valid consideration for B's promise to do the same. The consideration (the £100) moves from the promisee (A) at the request of the promisor (B). The fact that it moves to C rather than B is irrelevant. Therefore A can enforce B's promise and *vice versa*. However, C cannot enforce either promise as he is not a party to the bargain: under the *doctrine of privity of contract*, a person who is not a party to the contract cannot accrue rights or incur obligations under it. This is sometimes explained by saying that C is a stranger to the consideration.

(c) consideration must be sufficient but need not be adequate. 'Sufficient' here means *something of value*, however small or trivial. There is no requirement that it be of equal value to that which is being given in return. The law is only concerned with the existence of the bargain, not its quality (*Thomas v. Thomas* (1842); *Chappell & Co Ltd v. Nestle Co Ltd* (1960)).

(d) consideration must not be past: past consideration is no consideration (*Roscorla v. Thomas* (1842); *Re McArdle* (1951)).

For example, A cleans B's windows and B later promises to pay A £10 for doing so. A cannot enforce B's promise to pay because his consideration (the window cleaning) was already past when B made the promise.

There are two difficult areas regarding consideration:

(a) Can performance of an existing duty be valid consideration for a later agreement?

This depends on the origin of the existing duty:

(i) where the duty is one imposed by the general law, performance of that duty can only be valid consideration where the performance *exceeds* that required by law. It is this additional element which forms the consideration for the later agreement (*Collins v. Godefroy* (1831); *Glasbrook Bros Ltd v. Glamorgan County Council* (1925)).

(ii) where the duty is imposed by an earlier contract with the *same* party, performance of that duty will again be valid consideration for the later agreement where it exceeds that required by the earlier one (*Stilk v. Myrick* (1809); *Hartley v. Ponsonby* (1857)). However, it has been held that mere re-affirmation of an earlier promise may be valid consideration where the re-affirmation is a benefit to the promisee, *provided* the later agreement was not the result of fraud or economic duress (*Williams v. Roffey Bros & Nicholls (Contractors) Ltd* (1991)).

(iii) where the duty is imposed by an earlier contract with a *different* party, performance of that duty may be valid consideration for a later agreement (*Scotson v. Pegg* (1861); *New Zealand Shipping Co Ltd v. A M Satterthwaite & Co Ltd (The Eurymedon)* (1975)).

(b) Can a promise to pay part of a debt be valid consideration for a promise to release from the remainder?

Under the rule in *Pinnel's Case* (1602), this *is not* valid consideration. However, there are a number of exceptions to the rule:

(i) part-payment at the creditor's request before the date the debt is due is valid consideration. The earlier payment provides additional and fresh consideration;

(ii) part-payment at the creditor's request at a different place is similarly valid;

(iii) part-payment at the creditor's request together with some goods, or settlement by goods alone is similarly valid;

(iv) the rule does not apply where the amount is disputed. The consideration is the risk of paying more than is in fact due;

(v) the rule does not apply where the smaller sum is paid by a third party. To allow the creditor to go back on his promise would be a fraud on that third party (*Hirachand Punamchand v. Temple* (1911));

(vi) the rule does not apply where the debtor has entered into a composition agreement with his creditors. Under this type of agreement, all the creditors agree to accept a dividend (so much in the pound) in full settlement of their claims. Again, to allow one creditor to go back on this agreement would amount to a fraud on the others (*Wood v. Robarts* (1818)).

Promissory estoppel: despite these limitations on the rule in *Pinnel's Case*, there may still be circumstances where the common law rule applies yet it would be unjust to allow the creditor to go back on his promise. In such circumstances, the debtor may be able to rely on the equitable doctrine of promissory estoppel: where the debtor has acted in reliance on the creditor's promise, the court may exercise its discretion to estop (prevent) the creditor going back on that promise even though the debtor has provided no consideration (*Central London Property Trust Ltd v. High Trees House Ltd* (1947)).

Unilateral contracts

As indicated above, slightly different rules regarding offer, acceptance and consideration apply in relation to unilateral contracts. A unilateral contract arises where one party has made a conditional offer—for example, an offer of reward. If A offers a £50 reward to anyone who finds and returns his lost dog (the condition), then he is bound to pay that reward to anyone who fulfils that condition. Therefore, while advertisements are generally regarded as invitations to treat, an advertisement of reward will usually be held to be a conditional offer (*Carlill v. Carbolic Smoke Ball Co* (1893)). However, unilateral contracts are rare, and largely limited to contracts of reward and analogous circumstances.

Once a conditional offer has been made, acceptance is effective (in that the offer cannot be revoked) as soon as someone begins to perform the condition (*Errington v. Errington and Woods* (1952)), and the offeror is held to have waived the requirement of communication (*Carlill*). However, the offeror will be released from his obligations if performance of the condition is begun but not completed. While partial performance is sufficient acceptance to prevent revocation, only full performance will amount to consideration.

Intention

For the bargain to be a contract, the parties must have intended it to give rise to legal obligations. In deciding whether this was the case, the courts are guided by two presumptions:

(a) **social and domestic agreements:** here no contractual intention is presumed (for example, in agreements between husband and wife) (*Balfour v. Balfour* (1919)). However, this presumption may be rebutted by clear evidence to the contrary (for example, where the husband and wife have separated) (*Merritt v. Merritt* (1970)).

(b) **business and commercial agreements:** here a contractual intention is presumed, though this may again be rebutted by clear evidence to the contrary (for example, through the use of 'honour clauses') (*Rose & Frank Co v. J R Crompton & Bros Ltd* (1923)). There is also a statutory reversal of this presumption regarding collective bargaining agreements in industry (Trade Union and Labour Relations Act 1974, s.18).

Capacity

The parties must have the legal capacity to enter into contractual relations. While most people have full contractual capacity, the law does place restrictions on the capacity of certain groups, in order to protect them from exploitation:

The mentally disordered: where a person, at the time of making a contract, is suffering from a mental disorder which prevents them understanding the nature or significance of the arrangement, then he may subsequently avoid the contract, *provided* the other party was or ought to have been aware of the disorder at the time the contract was made (*Molton v. Camroux* (1848)). This applies to all contracts *except* contracts for necessary services (*Re Rhodes* (1890)) and goods (Sale of Goods Act 1979, s.3), where the disordered party may be required to pay a *reasonable price* for them. A reasonable price is not necessarily the same as the contract price, thus still providing protection against exploitation.

Drunkards: drunkards are given the same protection and are in the same position as the mentally disordered (*Gore v. Gibson* (1845); Sale of Goods Act 1979, s.3).

Minors: minors' (those under 18) contracts fall into three categories:

(a) **valid:** a minor is bound by contracts for necessary services (*Chapple v. Cooper* (1844)) and goods (*Nash v. Inman* (1908); Sale of Goods Act 1979, s.3) to pay a reasonable price for them. 'Necessaries' are goods and services which are suitable *both* to the condition in life of the minor *and* to his actual requirements at the time the contract was made. Therefore, a minor will only be bound where the contract is for goods or services which not only might be regarded as necessary (given his status and lifestyle) but also which he actually needed at the time.

A minor is also bound by beneficial contracts of employment

(*Doyle v. White City Stadium* (1935))—for example, a contract of apprenticeship.

(b) **voidable:** a minor can subsequently avoid a contract concerning interests in land (for example, a lease), a contract to purchase shares or a contract of partnership.

(c) **void:** these are contracts which can neither be enforced by the minor nor be enforced against him, and include contracts for non-necessary goods and services and contracts of loan. The position regarding such contracts is regulated by the Minors' Contracts Act 1987. Section 2 provides that any guarantee of a loan made by an adult guarantor can be enforced notwithstanding that the contract of loan itself is void. Section 3 provides that the courts may order the return of non-necessary goods or any identifiable proceeds of their sale.

b. Vitiating Factors

While the presence of the five characteristics outlined above give rise to a *prima facie* valid contract, there may be other factors at work which either undermine that validity (making the contract *voidable*) or destroy it entirely (making the contract *void*):

Void contracts: where a contract is void *ab initio* (from the outset), the general rule is that the parties must be returned to their pre-contractual positions. This is known as *restitution*. Therefore, any money or goods which have changed hands must be returned. Where this is not possible (for example, where the goods have been consumed or the contract was for a service which has been performed), the court may order payment in quasi-contract on a *quantum meruit* (as much as it is worth) basis.

Voidable contracts: where the contract is voidable, the party wishing to avoid it can apply for the equitable remedy of *rescission*. Again, the aim is to return the parties to their pre-contractual position. As with all equitable remedies, rescission is discretionary and the courts will *not* grant it:

(a) where the party seeking to rescind the contract has previously affirmed it, *i.e.* has continued to perform the contract in the knowledge that it was voidable. Delay in seeking rescission does not, in itself, amount to affirmation but may be regarded as such where rescission would be unreasonable after such a lapse of time (this would be an example of the application of the maxim 'delay defeats Equity').

(b) where restitution (or *restitutio in integrum*) is not possible (see above, p. 88). The courts do not insist on precise restitution: it is sufficient that the goods be returned in *substantially* the same state as that in which they were received.

(c) where a third party has acquired rights in the subject matter of the contract in good faith and for value.

There are six main vitiating factors which will make a contract either void or voidable:

Lack of required formality

Most contracts are 'simple' contracts, meaning that there are no formal requirements to be met in creating one. However, some contracts (such as those concerning interests in land or shares) must be made in writing or evidenced in writing in order to be valid.

Duress and undue influence

Where a person has been pressurised into entering a contract, that contract will be voidable (*Pao On v. Lau Yiu Long* (1980)). There are two forms of pressure recognised by law:

(a) **duress:** originally, the common law notion of duress only applied where the pressure took the form of physical violence to the person or the threat of such violence. More recently, it has been expanded to include commercial pressure (or 'economic duress') (*Universe Tankships Inc of Monrovia v. International Transport Workers Federation, The Universe Sentinel* (1983)).

(b) undue influence: the equitable doctrine of undue influence recognises more subtle forms of pressure and also the abuse of a privileged position of influence. A presumption of undue influence arises where the parties were in a special fiduciary relationship (or relationship of trust); for example, doctor and patient, solicitor and client.

Illegality

A contract will be void if it is illegal either in its objective or manner of performance; for example, contracts to commit a crime, tort or fraud, contracts to promote sexual immorality, contracts to promote corruption in public life, contracts of trade with an enemy in wartime. Where a contract is void for illegality, the general position is that any goods or money transferred are *not* recoverable (*Parkinson v. College of Ambulance Ltd and Harrison* (1925)).

Contrary to public policy

Contracts contrary to public policy are void; for example, contracts prejudicial to the institution of marriage, contracts in unreasonable restraint of trade, gaming and wagering contracts.

Mistake

There are rare occasions where a mistake by one of the parties will make the contract void:

(a) mistake as to the subject matter: where one party believes the contract to be about one thing and the other party believes it to be about something different, then there is no real agreement and the contract will be void (*Raffles v. Wichelhaus* (1864)). However, where the parties believe they are contracting about the same thing and are merely mistaken as to its quality, the contract will be valid.

(b) **mistake as to the existence of the subject matter:**
where, unknown to the parties, the subject matter of the contract has ceased to exist prior to the contract being made, that contract will be void (*Strickland v. Turner* (1852)). Where the subject matter ceases to exist after agreement but before performance, the contract may be frustrated (see below, p. 96).

(c) **mistake as to the person:** where one party is mistaken as to the identity of the other party, this will only make the contract void where the precise identity of the person is relevant to the decision to enter into the contract (*Cundy v. Lindsay* (1878)).

Misrepresentation

Where a statement made during contractual negotiations does not become a term of the contract, it remains a pre-contractual representation. If that statement were untrue, it would be a misrepresentation, and the misrepresentee may have a remedy against the misrepresentor. Whether this is the case depends upon:

(a) **the nature of the representation:** it must be a statement of fact, not of law, opinion or intention.

Generally, it must be a positive statement. Silence will not amount to misrepresentation (*Fletcher v. Krell* (1873)) except in three circumstances:

(i) where the representor fails to inform the representee of a change in circumstance which makes a previously true statement false (*With v. O'Flanagan* (1936));

(ii) where the representation, although literally true, leaves out important information which thereby creates a false impression (*Nottingham Patent Brick & Tile Co v. Butler* (1996));

(iii) where the contract is one of the utmost good faith (for example, an insurance contract).

(b) **the nature of the inducement:** a misrepresentation is only operative where it induces the misrepresentee to enter into a contract with the misrepresentor. Therefore the representee must show that he relied on the truth of the statement in making that decision. Where he has carried out independent investigations into its truth, there is no such reliance (*Attwood v. Small* (1838)). Where, however, the representee has the opportunity to carry out such investigations but declines to do so, then there is reliance on the statement (*Redgrave v. Hurd* (1881)). While the representation must be a factor in the representee's decision, it need not be the sole factor (*Edgington v. Fitzmaurice* (1885)).

(c) **the nature of the misrepresentation:** there are three types of misrepresentation:
  (i) **fraudulent:** this is where the representor makes the statement knowing it to be false, believing it to be false or being reckless as to its truth (*Derry v. Peek* (1889));
  (ii) **negligent:** this is where the representor believes the statement to be true but that belief is unreasonable;
  (iii) **innocent:** this is where the representor believes the statement to be true and that belief is reasonable.

The consequences of misrepresentation: an operative misrepresentation makes the contract voidable. The remedies available to the misrepresentee depend upon the type of misrepresentation:

(a) **fraudulent:** damages (in the tort of deceit) **and** rescission.

(b) **negligent:** damages (under section 2(1) of the Misrepresentation Act 1967) **and** rescission (or damages in lieu under section 2(2) of the 1967 Act).

(c) **innocent:** rescission (or damages in lieu under section 2(2) of the 1967 Act).

c. The Terms Of The Contract

It is the terms of the contract that define the rights and duties of the parties to it. These terms may be classified in two ways:

(a) by status: classifying contractual terms by their status creates three categories:

   (i) **conditions:** these are the most significant or important terms. They define the principal rights and duties of the parties. They are central to or lie at the heart of the contract.

   (ii) **warranties:** these are the less significant or minor terms. They identify the secondary rights and duties of the parties, and lie at the periphery of the contract.

   (iii) **innominate terms:** these are terms whose status or importance is unclear and which can only be decided in light of the consequences of the term being breached.

(b) by origin: classifying contractual terms by their origin creates two categories:

   (i) **express terms:** these are terms expressly stated by the parties themselves.

   (ii) **implied terms:** these are terms implied into the contract by law, either by common law or statute. At common law, the courts are reluctant to interfere in the nature of the contract as decided by the paties. Therefore, they will only imply a term where it is *both* reasonable *and* obvious and necessary to give business efficacy or make commercial sense of the contract (*The Moorcock* (1889); *Liverpool City Council v. Irwin* (1977)). The most obvious source of such implied terms is commercial custom and practice (*Hutton v. Warren* (1836)). Regarding statute, a number of Acts of Parliament imply terms into contracts; for example, the Sale of Goods Act 1979 (as amended) and the Supply of Goods and Services Act 1982 (as amended).

A problematic term: the exclusion or limitation clause

These are terms of the contract which seek to exclude or limit liability for breach of contract. While the use of such clauses is, in principle, perfectly legitimate, the law has recognised that they are open to abuse by parties in a dominant bargaining position. This is particularly so where they are included in *standard form contracts* which are offered on a 'take it or leave it' basis. Accordingly, exclusion and limitation clauses are subject to both judicial and statutory regulation:

(a) **Judicial regulation:** the courts have developed two main controls over the use of exclusion clauses:

    (i) **incorporation:** to be effective, the exclusion clause must have been properly incorporated into the contract. This means the other party must have been given reasonably sufficient notice of the clause (*Parker v. South Eastern Railway Co* (1877)) at or before the time the contract was made (*Olley v. Marlborough Court Ltd* (1949); *Thornton v. Shoe Lane Parking Ltd* (1971)).

    (ii) **construction:** to be effective, the clause must, upon proper construction (or interpretation), cover the breach which has occurred. In construing exclusion clauses, the courts are guided by two important principles:

(a) *the contra proferentem rule*: where there is any doubt or ambiguity in the clause, this will be resolved against the party seeking to rely on it. In other words, the benefit of any doubt is given to the injured party (*Baldry v. Marshall* (1925)); *Andrews v. Singer* (1934)).

(b) *the main purpose rule*: it is presumed that no exclusion clause is intended to defeat the main purpose of the contract by excluding liability for failing to fulfil that purpose (*Glynn v. Margetson & Co* (1893)). Nevertheless, this presumption may be rebutted by sufficiently strong and clear words (*Suisse Atlantique Société d'Armement Maritime SA v. Roterrdamsche Kolen Centrale NV* (1967); *Photo Production Ltd v. Securicor Transport Ltd* (1980)).

(b) **Statutory regulation:** while the courts are able to place significant restrictions on the use of exclusion clauses, the common law cannot prohibit their use. It was this (among other considerations) which prompted the enactment of the Unfair Contract Terms Act 1977. This Act places an absolute prohibition on the effectiveness of some exclusion clauses, and subjects others to a strict test of reasonableness (for a more detailed discussion of the Act, see below, p. 106).

d. Discharge of Contract

A contract may be discharged (brought to an end) in four ways.

Performance

The vast majority of contracts are discharged perfectly satisfactorily by each party performing their obligations. The general rule is that each party must perform his obligations *exactly* and *entirely*, otherwise they will be in breach and will forfeit any rights under the contract. However, this rule may operate very harshly in some circumstances, and the law has developed a number of significant exceptions to it:

   (i) **severable contracts:** where the contract consists of obligations which can be subdivided (for example, to carry freight at so much per ton), then a party may claim for those elements performed while remaining liable for breach of those not performed (*Ritchie v. Atkinson* (1808); *Atkinson v. Ritchie* (1809)).

   (ii) **prevention of performance:** where one party is prevented from performing his obligations by the other party, that failure of performance will not bar that party from bringing an action for breach of contract by the other party (*Planche v. Colburn* (1831)).

   (iii) **acceptance of partial performance:** where one party has partially performed his obligations and the other party has accepted this, this may be regarded as the abandonment of the original contract and the creation of a new, less extensive one. However, this will only apply where the other party has a genuine choice as to whether to accept the partial performance (*Sumpter v. Hedges* (1898)).

   (iv) **substantial performance:** where one party has substantially performed their obligations, then they may enforce the contract *subject* to a reduction to compensate for the defect in performance (*Hoenig v. Isaacs* (1952)). This only applies where the defect in performance is minor; *i.e.* where the other party has still received a substantial benefit (*Bolton v. Mahadeva* (1972)).

   (v) **tender of performance:** where one party tender (or

offers) performance and this is rejected by the other party, the tender is regarded as equivalent to performance. This exception does not apply where the obligation is one to make payment: an unsuccessful tender of payment does not release the person of the obligation to pay.

Agreement

The parties to the contract can agree to vary or discharge it. As such an agreement amounts to a contract to end a contract, it must be supported by fresh consideration.

Frustration

Generally, contractual liability is strict, in that it is not necessary to show that the party in breach was at fault in their failure to perform. However, the doctrine of frustration is one area of non-performance where fault (or rather the absence of fault) does play a part. In *Taylor v. Caldwell* (1863), it was held that where performance of the contract had become impossible and neither party was at fault, then both parties were discharged from any further obligations under that contract. This position has subsequently developed into the modern doctrine of frustration:

> **The parties to a contract are released from any further obligations under that contract where an unforeseen event occurs which makes further performance either:**
> **(a) impossible**
> **(b) illegal**
> **(c) radically different from that anticipated by both parties at the time the contract was made**
> **and the frustrating event was not the fault of either party.**

These three variations require further explanation:

(a) **impossibility:** subsequent impossibility of performance may occur in three ways:
>   (i) where the subject matter is destroyed (*Taylor v. Caldwell* (1863));

(ii) where the subject matter becomes unavailable (*Jackson v. Union Marine Insurance Co Ltd* (1874); *Morgan v. Manser* (1948));

(iii) where, in a contract for personal services, one of the parties dies.

(b) illegality: where a subsequent event (for example, new legislation or the outbreak of war) makes further performance illegal, the contract will be frustrated (*Fibrosa Spolka Akcyjna v. Fairburn Lawson Combe Barber Ltd* (1943)).

(c) radical difference: where further performance would produce a result radically different from that anticipated by both parties at the time the contract was made, the contract will be frustrated (*Krell v. Henry* (1903); *Herne Bay Steamboat Co v. Hutton* (1903)). To amount to a radical difference, the actual and anticipated results of performance must be almost totally different; for example, events which would lead to a reduction in anticipated profits will not frustrate the contract (*Davis Contractors Ltd v. Fareham UDC* (1956)).

A party cannot plead frustration where the frustrating event is due to their own fault, *i.e.* the frustration must not be self-induced (*Maritime National Fish Ltd v. Ocean Trawlers Ltd* (1935)).

The consequences of frustration: while the question as to whether a contract has been frustrated remains an issue of common law, the consequences of frustration are now regulated by the Law Reform (Frustrated Contracts) Act 1943:

(a) frustration immediately discharges the contract and releases the parties from any further obligations under it (section 1(1)).

(b) any money paid prior to the frustrating event can be recovered (section 1(2));

(c) any money due to be paid prior to the frustrating event, but not in fact paid, ceases to be payable (section 1(2));

(d) expenses incurred under the contract may be recovered up to the amount of sums paid or due to be paid prior to the frustrating event (section 1(2)). If no sums had been paid

or were due to be paid, then no expenses may be recovered;
(e) a party that has acquired a valuable benefit under the contract prior to the frustrating event may be ordered to pay a reasonable sum for it, whether or not any sums had been paid or were due to be paid (section 1(3)).

This allows the court to apportion any loss resulting from the frustration in a fair way.

Breach

Breach of contract may take two forms:

(a) **actual breach:** where a party fails to perform any or all of their obligations (non-performance) or performs them improperly (defective performance).

(b) **anticipatory breach:** where a party gives a clear indication of an intention not to perform their obligations. This gives rise to an immediate cause of action (*Hochster v. De la Tour* (1853)).

The consequences of breach depend upon the status of the term breached:

(a) **breach of condition:** gives the injured party a right to damages and the option to repudiate (treat as discharged) the contract (*Heyman v. Darwins Ltd* (1942)). This is sometimes referred to as repudiatory breach.

(b) **breach of warranty:** gives the injured party a right to damages *only*. They remain bound to fulfil their own obligations under the contract. This is sometimes referred to as mere breach.

(c) **breach of an innominate term:** here the rights of the injured party depend upon the consequences of the breach

(*Cehave NV v. Bremer Handelsgesellschaft GmbH, The Hansa Nord* (1976)). If the breach substantially deprives the injured party of his anticipated contractual benefits, it will be regarded as a breach of condition. Where the consequences are less severe, it will be treated as a breach of warranty.

e. Remedies for Breach of Contract

At common law, the only remedy is that of damages. In exceptional circumstances, the equitable remedies of specific performance and the injunction may be available for breach of contract.

Damages

The aim of damages (financial compensation) is to put the injured party, in so far as possible, in their *anticipated post-contractual* position (*Robinson v. Harman* (1848)). Put another way, damages are intended to compensate the injured party for any loss suffered as a result of the breach of contract.

A claim for damages may take two forms:

(a) **liquidated damages:** this is where the parties have provided for compensation in the contract itself, either by specifying the amount of damages to be paid or a formula for working them out (for example, a cancellation charge clause in a package holiday contract). Liquidated damage clauses are valid *provided* they are a genuine attempt to pre-estimate the likely loss resulting from the breach.

However, a dominant party may misuse such a clause to introduce penalties into the contract designed to ensure performance by the weaker party. If the courts decide the clause is a penalty clause, it will be struck out and the claim treated as one for unliquidated damages (see below). Therefore, the courts will regard it as a penalty clause where (*Dunlop Pneumatic Tyre Co Ltd v. New Garage & Motor Co Ltd* (1915)):

   (i) the sum specified is clearly greater than any conceivable or likely loss;
   (ii) the breach is a failure to pay sums due and the damages specified exceed that sum;

(iii) the same sum is specified for a number of breaches, some of which are trivial and some serious.

(b) **unliquidated damages:** where there is no liquidated damages clause, the claim will be for unliquidated damages and will be assessed according to the principles established in *Hadley v. Baxendale* (1854) (and confirmed in *The Heron II* (1969)). Under these principles, the injured party may recover damages in respect of:

(i) losses which are a natural consequence of the breach;

(ii) losses which, though not a natural consequence of the breach, were either known or ought to have been known to be a possibility by both parties at the time the contract was made.

Two further points regarding the assessment of damages should be noted:

(a) **speculation:** that fact that the loss may be difficult to quantify is no bar to recovery. The court may engage in a degree of speculation in estimating the loss (*Chaplin v. Hicks* (1911)).

(b) **mitigation:** the injured party must take reasonable steps to mitigate (keep to a minimum) their losses. They cannot recover for losses due to their own unreasonable failure to mitigate (*British Westinghouse Electric & Manufacturing Co Ltd v. Underground Electric Railways Co of London Ltd* (1912)).

Specific performance

This is a court order instructing the party in breach to perform their contractual obligations. As with all equitable remedies, specific performance is discretionary and (with the exception of contracts concerning interests in land) is rarely awarded. It will not be awarded where:

(a) damages are an adequate remedy. For example, in a contract for the sale of goods, specific performance will not be

awarded unless the goods are unique (*Cohen v. Roche* (1927));
(b) the contract lacks mutuality, *i.e.* where the remedy would not be available to both parties (for example, contracts with minors) (*Flight v. Bolland* (1828));
(c) the order would require constant supervision (*Ryan v. Mutual Tontine Westminster Chambers Association* (1893));
(d) the contract is one for personal services (*Rigby v. Connol* (1880)).

Where an application for specific performance is refused, the court may award damages in lieu.

Injunctions

A prohibitory injunction may be granted to prevent a breach of an express negative contractual obligation (for example, a valid restraint of trade clause (*Lumley v. Wagner* (1852); *Warner Bros Pictures Inc v. Nelson* (1937)). However, this will not be done where the consequence would be to compel performance of other positive obligations for which specific performance would be unobtainable (*Page One Records v. Britton* (1967)). Again, the court may award damages in lieu where an injunction is refused.

2. FREEDOM OF CONTRACT AND CONSUMER PROTECTION

Introduction

The main period of development for English contract law was during the nineteenth century. During this time, the great expansion in trade that took place was accompanied by significant developments in the law that facilitated that trade. The prevailing economic philosophy of the time was one of *laissez-faire* or free trade. Consequently, state intervention in, and regulation of, economic activity was kept to a minimum. For the law of contract, this meant that the role of the law was simply to act as an agent for the enforcement of individual agreements, freely arrived at. It was not for the law to intervene and dictate the content of such bargains. Hence, the notion of freedom of contract assumed a central importance. Necessarily allied to this notion was the concept of equality of bargaining power. The law assumed the parties to a contract approached negotiations from positions of approximately equal bargaining strength. Therefore, if one party displayed less business acumen and skill and agreed to a relatively disadvantageous contract, he could not turn to the law to save himself from the consequences of his own commercial ineptitude.

While this view was, arguably, consistent with the realities of an emerging industrial capitalist economy, it has become increasingly outdated and unrealistic in a modern, complex, multinational, post-industrial economy. The idea of equality of bargaining power has become, even in many business to business transactions, little more than a fiction. In many instances today, one party will approach negotiations from a position of strength or dominance over the other. This clearly leaves the weaker party vulnerable to unfair exploitation. In order to prevent this, it has become increasingly necessary for the law to adopt a more regulatory and interventionist position. Therefore, the development of the law of contract in the twentieth century has represented, particularly with regard to consumer transactions, an orderly and steady retreat from the idea of freedom of contract.

It should be noted, however, that English law has never acknowledged absolute freedom of contract. It has always intervened to protect vulnerable groups (for example, through the rules regarding contractual capacity and the operation of duress and undue influence as vitiating factors). It has always also exercised a degree of regulation in the public interest (for example, through the operation of illegality and public policy as vitiating factors). As equality of bargaining power has declined, the law has simply been forced to recognise new vulnerable groups (for example, consumers, employees and tenants) and new areas of public interest (for example, through fair trading and monopolies and mergers legislation).

It should also be noted that, with regard to consumer transactions, intervention in freedom of contract is only one of the methods used by the law to protect the weaker party:

(a) legislation has been used to ensure consumers are provided with full and accurate information before entering into a contract (Trade Descriptions Act 1968; Consumer Credit Act 1974; Consumer Protection Act 1987).

(b) legislation has also sought to ensure that consumer products are safe to use (the Consumer Safety Acts; Consumer Protection Act 1987; and various subordinate safety regulations).

(c) a general regulatory framework has been established under the Fair Trading Act 1973, and various forms of licensing are sometimes used to regulate traders (for example, in the consumer credit field).

(d) the Director General of Fair Trading has a statutory duty (under section 124(3) of the Fair Trading Act 1973) to encourage business self-regulation through trade association codes of practice.

Therefore, the law has taken a number of significant measures in recent years to redress the growing contractual inequality between trader and consumer and to protect the consumer from unfair exploitation.

Legislative Intervention In Freedom Of Contract

Three Acts of Parliament are of particular concern here:

The Sale Of Goods Act 1979 (as amended by the Sale and Supply of Goods Act 1994)

The provisions of this Act apply to all contracts for the sale of goods, *i.e.* contracts where the ownership of goods is exchanged for money (s.2(1)). The Act then goes on to imply up to four important terms into such contracts for the protection of the buyer:

(a) **the implied condition as to title (s.12)**;
  (b) **the implied condition as to correspondence with description (s.13)**;
  (c) **the implied condition as to satisfactory quality (s.14)**;
  (d) **the implied condition as to correspondence with sample (s.15)**.

There are, therefore, a number of issues which must be addressed when considering the application of the Act:

(a) it must be determined whether the contract is one to which the Act applies. This is done by applying the definition in section 2.

(b) Section 12 implies into *all* contracts for the sale of goods a condition that the seller has the right to sell the goods.
(c) where the sale is a sale by description, section 13 implies a condition that the goods must correspond with that description. For example, if an overcoat is described (by whatever means) as being '100 per cent pure new wool', it must in fact be 100 per cent pure new wool.
(d) where the seller is selling in the course of a business (*i.e.* the sale is not a private sale), section 14(2) implies a general requirement that the goods be of a satisfactory quality, *i.e.* of the standard a reasonable person would regard as satisfactory (s.14(2A)).

This applies to goods of any type. Any description, such as 'seconds', 'sale goods', 'second-hand', and any reduction in price are merely factors to be taken into consideration in deciding whether or not the goods are of satisfactory quality (s.14(2A)).

Section 14(2B) provides that 'quality' includes not only functional characteristics (such as fitness for common purpose, freedom from minor defects, safety and durability) but also cosmetic characeristics (such as appearance and finish), together with the general state and condition of the goods.

However, section 14(2C) provides that this general requirement does not apply to:
(i) defects which were specifically drawn to the buyer's attention before the contract was made.
(ii) defects which a reasonable examination of the goods would have revealed, *provided* the buyer did in fact examine the goods before the contract was made.

The general requirement refers only to goods being fit for their *common* purpose. Section 14(3), however, provides that where the buyer makes known to the seller any *particular* purpose (whether common or not) for which the goods are being bought, then the goods must be fit for that purpose *unless* the seller can show either:
(i) that the buyer did not rely on the skill and judgment of the seller; or
(ii) if the buyer did so rely, that reliance was unreasonable in the circumstances.
(e) where the sale is a sale by sample, section 15 implies a condition that the bulk must correspond in quality to the sample.

Breach, acceptance and the loss of repudiation

The implied terms are expressly stated by the Act to be conditions. Therefore, any breach will, *prima facie*, be a repudiatory breach, entitling the buyer to reject the goods, repudiate the contract and claim damages. It has already been seen that the right to repudiate may be lost (for example, where *restitutio in integrum* is not possible). Section 11 of the Act provides that the right to repudiate is also lost where the buyer has 'accepted' the goods. Section 35 provides that goods have been accepted where:

    (a) the buyer indicates to the seller that he has accepted them.

    (b) the buyer does some act in relation to the goods that is inconsistent with the ownership of the seller. However, it should be noted that using the goods in order to discover whether they conform to the requirements of the contract (*i.e.* that they work) does *not* amount to acceptance of them.

    (c) the buyer keeps the goods beyond a reasonable time without indicating to the seller that he intends to reject them. Therefore, the buyer should notify the seller promptly of any defect and any intention to reject the goods.

    (d) simply asking for or agreeing to the repair of the goods does not amount to acceptance. If the goods are still unsatisfactory following 'repair', the buyer may still be able to reject them.

Exclusion of liability

Section 55 provides that liability for breach of the implied terms can be limited or excluded, *subject to* the provisions of the Unfair Contract Terms Act 1977.

The Supply Of Goods And Services Act 1982 (as amended by the Sale and Supply of Goods Act 1994)

The provisions of this Act apply to three types of contract:

(a) **contracts for the transfer of goods:** where the ownership of goods is exchanged for something other than money (s.1);

(b) **contracts for the hire of goods:** where the possession of goods is transferred for a specified period (s.6);

(c) **contracts for the supply of a service:** where a service is provided (other than under a contract of employment) (s.12).

Regarding contracts for the transfer of goods, the Act implies terms (similar to those of the 1979 Act) as to title (s.2), correspondence with description (s.3), satisfactory quality (s.4) and correspondence with sample (s.5).

Regarding contracts for the hire of goods, the Act implies terms (again similar to the 1979 Act) as to the hirer's right to transfer possession of the goods (s.7), correspondence with description (s.8), satisfactory quality (s.9) and correspondence with sample (s.10).

Regarding contracts for the supply of a service, the Act implies the following terms:

(a) where the supplier is acting in the course of a business, that the service will be carried out with reasonable care and skill (s.13).

(b) where the supplier is acting in the course of a business, and unless otherwise provided for in the contract, the service will be carried out within a reasonable time (s.14).

(c) unless otherwise provided for in the contract, the person contracting with the supplier will pay a reasonable price for the service (s.15).

Finally, section 11 (regarding the transfer and hire of goods) and section 16 (regarding the supply of a service) provide that liability for breach of the implied terms may be excluded or restricted *subject to* the provisions of the Unfair Contract Terms Act 1977.

The Unfair Contract Terms Act 1977

The relationship between this Act and the 1979 and 1982 Acts must now be considered:

(a) Section 2 of the 1977 Act regulates attempts to limit or exclude business liability (whether contractual or tortious) for negligence. Such liability for causing death or personal injury *cannot* be limited or excluded (s.2(1)). Negligence liability for causing other forms of loss or damage *can* be excluded or restricted, but only in so far as the term is *reasonable*. These constraints apply to attempts to exclude or restrict liability for breach of the implied term in contracts for the supply of a service as to reasonable care and skill under section 13 of the 1982 Act.

(b) Section 6 of the 1977 Act regulates attempts to exclude or restrict liability for breach of the implied terms in contracts for the sale of goods under the 1979 Act:

(i) liability for breach of the implied condition as to title (s.12, 1979) *cannot* be excluded or restricted;

(ii) as against a *consumer*, liability for breach of the implied terms as to correspondence with description (s.13, 1979), satisfactory quality (s.14, 1979) and correspondence with sample (s.15, 1979) *cannot* be excluded or restricted;

(iii) as against a *non-consumer*, liability for breach of the implied terms detailed in (ii) above *can* be excluded or restricted, but only in so far as the term is *reasonable*.

(c) Section 7 of the 1977 Act regulates attempts to exclude or restrict liability for breach of the implied terms in contracts for the transfer or hire of goods under the 1982 Act:

(i) liability for breach of the implied term in contracts for the transfer of goods as to title (s.2, 1982) *cannot* be excluded or restricted.

(ii) as against a *consumer*, liability for breach of the implied terms in contracts for the transfer of goods as to correspondence with description (s.3, 1982), satisfactory quality (s.4, 1982) and correspondence with sample (s.5, 1982) *cannot* be excluded or restricted.

(iii) as against a *non-consumer*, liability for breach of the implied terms detailed in (ii) above *can* be excluded or restricted, but only in so far as the term is *reasonable*.

(iv) liability for breach of the implied term in contracts for the hire of goods as to the right to transfer possession (s.7, 1982) *can* be excluded or restricted, but only in so far as the term is *reasonable*.

(v) as against a *consumer*, liability for breach of the implied terms in contracts for the hire of goods as to correspondence with description (s.8, 1982), satisfactory quality (s.9, 1982) and correspondence with sample (s.10, 1982) *cannot* be excluded or restricted.

(vi) as against a *non-consumer*, liability for breach of the implied detailed in (v) above *can* be excluded or restricted, but only in so far as the term is *reasonable*.

(d) Section 11 of the 1977 Act provides that a term is *reasonable* if can be considered fair and reasonable in the circumstances which were, or ought to have been, in the contemplation of both parties at the time the contract was made. Further explanation is given in Schedule 2 of the Act.

(e) Section 12 of the 1977 Act provides a definition of a *consumer* as being someone who is *not* dealing in the course of a business but who is contracting with someone who *is* dealing in the course of a business. Where the contract is one for the sale, supply or hire of goods, there is an additional requirement that the goods be of a type that is usually supplied for private use or consumption.

The Unfair Terms in Consumer Contracts Regulations 1994

These Regulations were introduced to implement the requirements of the European Directive on Unfair Terms, and extend beyond the control of exclusion clauses alone.

The Regulations apply to any consumer contract which has not been individually negotiated (*i.e.* it is a standard form contract) (Paragraph 3(1)).

Under Paragraph 5(1), any term which is deemed to be unfair will *not* be binding on the consumer.

Under Paragraph 4(1), a term is unfair where it causes a significant imbalance in the parties' rights and obligations under the contract to the detriment of the consumer.

Finally, Paragraph 6 requires sellers and suppliers to ensure that contracts are written in plain, intelligible language, and that where there is any doubt regarding the meaning of a term, the interpretation most favourable to the consumer is to be used.

Section Five: CRIMINAL LAW

1. GENERAL PRINCIPLES OF CRIMINAL LAW

It is difficult, if not impossible, to produce a comprehensive definition of a 'crime'. Commonly, people will think of crimes as acts which threaten public safety, security or morality. Alternatively, a crime can be defined as anti-social conduct which is sufficiently serious to require state intervention and punishment. While both these definitions account for the more serious offences against person and property, there are a number of acts (such as parking offences), and some omissions, which are subject to the criminal law and yet do not cause such a threat. Thus, to be accurate, one can only say that a crime is any act or omission which is contrary to the criminal law. While this identifies what conduct *is* a crime, it is of little help in identifying what conduct *ought* to be a crime.

Nevertheless, the 'popular' definition is useful in illustrating the general nature of criminal liability. One of the main reasons for having a criminal justice system is the belief that those who engage in antisocial conduct deserve to be held responsible for their actions and punished. In order to be deserving of punishment, a person must have acted in a blameworthy manner, *i.e.* have been in some way *at fault* in acting as they did. Though not a universal requirement, this notion of fault is a very important aspect of most criminal offences, and also helps to explain the basis of many of the defences to criminal liability. It is sensible, therefore, to keep this idea of fault or individual responsibility in mind throughout the discussion of the criminal law that follows.

The idea of fault is present in the principal maxim of the criminal law: *actus non facit reum nisi mens sit rea* (the act is not guilty unless the mind is also guilty). However, this maxim must be treated cautiously. As implied above, *mens rea* is not required for all criminal offences. Furthermore, the idea of a 'guilty mind' can be misleading: a person can have the required *mens rea* for a crime without being morally guilty, and *vice versa*.

However, most criminal offences contain both these elements: *actus reus* and *mens rea*. This means that for most crimes the prosecution must prove beyond a reasonable doubt that the accused person committed the *actus reus* of the crime, while at the same time having the required *mens rea*.

a. The actus reus

The term *actus reus* is best understood as meaning the **physical element** of a crime. It can include conduct, circumstance and consequence. For example, the *actus reus* of murder contains all three: an unlawful act (conduct), under the Queen's Peace (circumstances), which causes the death of another human being (consequence). By contrast, the *actus reus* of rape contains only two: sexual intercourse (either vaginal or anal penetration) (conduct), without the person's consent (circumstance). Thus, some offences, such as rape, are termed 'conduct' crimes, while others, such as murder, are termed 'consequence' or 'result' crimes.

Generally, the *actus reus* must be a voluntary positive act. An act is voluntary if it is consciously willed and deliberate. However, there are limited circumstances where an omission (rather than an act) will give rise to liability. The general position is that omissions do not attract criminal liability. For example, if A watches B (a complete stranger) drown and does nothing to save him, A has committed no crime. In these circumstances, A's omission is a *pure* omission. However, where a person has accepted a duty to act and then fails to do so, then liability may arise: the omission is no longer pure. This applies to both contractual (*R v. Pitwood* (1902)) and tortious (*R v. Stone and Dobinson* (1977)) duties. Legislation may also impose liability for omissions; for example, failing to report a road traffic accident.

Causation

An aspect of the *actus reus* that can cause problems is the requirement of causation. Where the *actus reus* consists of both conduct and consequence (*i.e.* it is a consequence or result crime), the prosecution must establish a clea and unbroken causal link between them; *i.e.* it must be proved that the accused's conduct caused the unlawful consequence. This is approached in two stages:

Cause in fact: the conduct must be a *sine qua non* of the consequence. This is established by applying the 'but for' test, showing that without the accused's conduct, the unlawful consequence would not have occurred. If the consequence would have occurred in any event, then it cannot be said to be the accused's fault. This applies even where the accused's conduct was intended, unsuccessfully, to cause the consequence (*R v. White* (1910)).

Cause in law: not every act which is a *sine qua non* of the consequence will attract criminal liability. In some circumstances, the conduct will be too remote (or distant) from the consequence, while in others the actions of a third party (known as a *novus actus interveniens*) will intervene and break the chain of causation. Thus, it is not sufficient to show that the accused's conduct was a factual cause of the unlawful consequence. It must also be a legal cause. The first point to note here is that the accused's conduct need not be the sole or even the main cause of the unlawful consequence (*R v. Pagett* (1983)). It is sufficient that it made a contribution. This raises the question as to what degree of contribution is required to give rise to liability. In *R v. Cheshire* (1991), it was stated that the accused's conduct must have made a 'significant contribution' in bringing about the unlawful consequence. The existence of a second cause will only break the causal link where its effect is so 'potent' that it makes the accused's contribution 'negligible'.

There are two further aspects of causation:

The accused must take his victim as he finds him: the accused cannot rely on some unusual characteristic of the victim (such as a weak heart) in order to avoid liability for the consequences of his conduct. This applies to both physical and psychological characteristics (*R v. Blaue* (1975)).

The accused will be held to have caused all the reasonably foreseeable consequences of his conduct: for example, where a person is threatened with an assault by the accused and, seeking to escape, injures themselves, the accused will be held to have caused those injuries *provided* the victim's attempt to escape was reasonably foreseeable (*R v. Pagett* (1983); *R v. Williams* (1992)). However, this only shows that the accused caused the consequence, not that he intended it. Intention is a state of mind and, therefore, is part of the mental element of the crime, not the physical.

and, therefore, is part of the mental element of the crime, not the physical.

b. The mens rea

The *mens rea* is the **mental element** of a crime. For most crimes, it is not sufficient to prove only that the accused committed the unlawful act. It must also be shown that they had a particular state of mind. The need to show a criminal state of mind emphasises the *subjective* nature of criminal liability and also highlights the central role of fault.

While the precise *mens rea* required varies from one offence to another, it will usually incorporate one of four general states of mind: intention; recklessness; negligence; and blameless inadvertence. Negligence and blameless inadvertence rarely give rise to criminal liability, and will be examined in the discussion of strict liability below. Therefore, discussion at this point will concentrate on intention and recklessness.

Intention: the issue here is whether or not the accused intended to bring about the unlawful consequence. The test for intention is as follows:

● a person *must* be held to intend a consequence where it is their *purpose* in acting to bring that consequence about (referred to as *direct* intent).
● a person *may* be held to intend a consequence where:
  (a) it was virtually certain to result from their actions; and
  (b) they knew it was virtually certain to result.
      (referred to as *oblique* intent).
      (*R v. Moloney* (1985); *R v. Hancock and Shankland* (1986); *R v Nedrick* (1986)).

That there is a *discretion* to infer intent in the latter circumstances is confirmed by section 8 of the Criminal Justice Act 1967.

Motive and desire: it is important to distinguish between intention/purpose and motive/desire. A person may intend a particular consequence without either desiring it or it being the motive for their actions. For example, so-called 'mercy' killings where a person gives an overdose of medication to a terminally-ill relative. Here, while they do not desire the death of their loved one, and their motive is to relieve suffering, they nevertheless intend to kill.

Proof of intention is always a sufficient condition of criminal liability. For some offences, such as murder, intention is also a necessary condition, *i.e. only* proof of intention is sufficient to give rise to liability.

Recklessness: a person is reckless where they take an unjustified risk of committing the offence. Whether or not a risk is justified is decided by an *objective* test, *i.e.* would a reasonable person regard the risk as unjustified (*R v. Lawrence* (1982); *R v. Sangha* (1988)). Therefore, the accused cannot avoid liability by arguing that in their *subjective* opinion, the risk was justified.

However, the accused's subjective perception of the risk is relevant in deciding whether criminal liability will flow from taking that risk. This emphasises once again the importance of individual fault and responsibility. The law has developed two different tests for recklessness:

'Cunningham' (or subjective) recklessness: under the test established in *R v. Cunningham* (1957), a person is reckless where:

    (a) he is subjectively aware of the existence of the risk; and

    (b) he nevertheless goes on to take that risk; and

    (c) the taking of the risk is objectively unjustified in the circumstances.

'Caldwell' (or objective) recklessness: under the test established in *R v. Caldwell* (1981), a person is reckless where:

    (a) the risk is a serious one; and

    (b) either

        (i) he is subjectively aware of the risk and nevertheless goes on to take it (essentially 'Cunningham' recklessness); or

        (ii) he gives no thought to the possibility of the risk and the risk was an obvious one; and

    (c) the taking of the risk is objectively unjustified under the circumstances.

While the 'Caldwell' test was at one point extended to include liability for manslaughter, concerns were frequently expressed regarding the undesirability of the second, objective limb ((ii) above) of the test. Following a period of judicial complexity and uncertainty, the decision in *R v. Adomako* (1994) once again limited the 'Caldwell' test to the offence of criminal damage (for which it was first introduced). For all other offences (except those which can only be committed intentionally), the 'Cunningham' test applies.

The relationship between the *actus reus* and *mens rea*

The requirement of coincidence: for liability to arise, the accused must have committed the *actus reus* while, at the same time, having formed the required *mens rea, i.e.* the criminal act and criminal state of mind must coincide. However, the courts have allowed a degree of flexibility in satisfying this requirement:

The 'continuing' offence: where the *actus reus* of the offence is of a continuing nature (for example, rape), it is sufficient that the accused forms the required *mens rea* at some point during its commission: the *mens rea* need not be present from the outset (*Fagan v. Metropolitan Police Commissioner* (1968)).

The 'transaction' principle: where the accused has committed a series of related acts (one of which is the *actus reus* of the offence), constituting a single *transaction*, it is sufficient that the accused forms the required *mens rea* at some point during this transaction (*Thabo Meli v. R* (1954); *R v. Church* (1965)). This applies even where there is an appreciable interval between the commission of the *actus reus* and formation of the *mens rea* (*R v. Le Brun* (1991)).

Transferred malice

The concept of transferred malice applies where a criminal act directed at one person or item of property results in injury, loss or damage to another person or item of property; for example, where A aims a blow at B but misses and strikes C instead. The malice toward the anticipated victim is transferred to the actual victim, thus preventing the accused from avoiding liability (*R v. Latimer* (1886)).

This concept will only apply where the anticipated and actual offence are of the same nature. Where this is not the case, the malice cannot be transferred; for example, where A throws a stone at B but misses and breaks C's window instead. However, it may be that in such circumstances, the accused will also have the required *mens rea* for the actual offence; in the above example, A may well have been reckless regarding the risk of damage to C's window.

Where the accused would have had a defence against the anticipated victim, this will also be transferred and operate against the actual victim (*R v. Gross* (1913)). For example, were A to aim a blow in self-defence at B but miss and strike C, A would be able to raise self-defence to any charge of assaulting C.

c. *General defences to criminal liability*

Proof of commission of the *actus reus* together with formation of the required *mens rea* will give rise to *prima facie* criminal liability. However, the accused may be able to rebut this *prima facie* case by establishing a defence. The operation of these defences again highlights the importance of fault as they show that the accused did not commit the *actus reus* voluntarily, or that he did not form the required *mens rea*, or that his actions were in some way justifiable or excusable.

Thus, these general defences operate in one of three ways:
- (a) by negating voluntary commission of the *actus reus*: non-insane automatism
- (b) by negating formation of the required *mens rea*: insanity
  mistake
  intoxication
  infancy
- (c) by way of justification or excuse: duress
  necessity
  self-defence
  (and its variations)
  consent of the victim

Non-insane automatism: Here, the accused argues that at the time of committing the *actus reus* he had no conscious, voluntary control over his actions: he was acting as an automaton. This is a defence because a person cannot be held to be at fault regarding conduct over which they had no control.

This defence is termed 'non-insane' automatism in order to distinguish it from the defence of insanity. The essential distinction between the two defences is that with non-insane automatism the cause of the automotive state must be *external* (such as medication or a blow to the head), while with insanity the cause must be *internal* (such as an illness or disease). For example, in *R v. Quick* (1973) a diabetic suffered a hypoglycaemic blackout because he had not taken his medication properly. As this was an external factor (the medication), conduct during the blackout was regarded as automatism. By contrast, in *R v. Hennessy* (1989), the blackout occurred when the diabetic had not taken his medication at all. Here, the blackout was attributed to an internal factor (the diabetes) and, hence, the appropriate defence was insanity. It should also be noted that, despite earlier dicta to the contrary, in *R v. Burgess* (1991) it was held that acts done while sleepwalking (in a state of somnambulism) were to be regarded as acts done while insane rather than under a state of automatism.

This defence is not available where the automotive state is self-induced through the voluntary consumption of dangerous drugs (*R v. Lipman* (1969)).

Insanity: Insanity, in this context, is a legal, *not* medical concept. It is designed to cover those situations where, because of some mental infirmity, the accused should not be held responsible for their actions. Where it is raised successfully, this defence does not result in an acquittal, but in a special verdict of 'not guilty by reason of insanity'. This allows the court considerable discretion in dealing with that person, ranging from an absolute discharge to detention in hospital (Criminal Procedure (Insanity and Unfitness to Plead) Act 1991).

This defence is governed by the M'Naghten Rules (established in *M'Nagten's Case* (1843)). The accused must show that, at the time of committing the offence, he was:

   (a) suffering from a defect of reason
   (b) that this was caused by a disease of the mind
   (c) with the result that either:
      (i) he did not know the nature and quality of his act; or
      (ii) if he did know this, he did not know that it was wrong.

Defect of reason: this means that the accused must have been totally deprived of the power to reason (*R v. Clarke* (1972)).

Disease of the mind: this is not limited to recognised mental illnesses, but includes any disease or internal factor which impairs mental function, and has been held to include arteriosclerosis (*R v. Kemp* (1957)), epilepsy (*R v. Sullivan* (1983)), diabetes (*R v. Hennessy* (1989)), and somnambulism (*R v. Burgess* (1991)). Thus, it is a far broader notion than simply mental illness or diseases of the brain.

Did not know the nature and quality of the act: this refers to the *physical* nature of the act, not its legal or moral status. This requirement is met where the accused is either acting as an unconscious automaton (as in *Kemp* where the arteriosclerosis caused a mental blackout) or where he was suffering from insane delusions (for example, cutting someone's throat under the delusion that he was slicing a loaf of bread).

Did not know that it was wrong: wrong, in this context, means contrary to law (*R v. Windle* (1952)). Thus, this requirement is met where the accused knew what he was doing, but he was suffering from insane delusions which, if true, would have made his conduct lawful (for example, where the accused kills in 'self-defence' while suffering from the delusion that the victim is an assassin sent to kill him).

The relationship between insanity and automatism

The distinction between automatism and insanity is important because while the former results in an acquittal, the latter results in the special verdict. The purpose (or policy) behind this distinction is to allow those whose mental condition does not represent a continuing danger to the public to go free, while permitting the detention of those who, though they are not criminally responsible for their actions, do remain a threat.

Unfortunately, the principles evolved to implement this policy (primarily the internal/external cause distinction) has led to some undesirable consequences; for example, the categorisation of conditions such as epilepsy and diabetes as insanity, and to some (arguably) unsustainable distinctions, for example, between the situations in *Quick* and *Hennessy*.

A better approach might be to have a single defence resulting in a special verdict of 'not guilty by reason of automatism', thereby allowing the court the discretion to deal with the individual in the most appropriate way, following consideration of medical and social reports. The courts have, however, made it clear that any such development must be legislative, rather than judicial (*R v. Sullivan* (1983)).

Mistake

A mistake of fact (but not of law) may operate as a defence where, as a result of the mistake, the accused did not form the required *mens rea*. For example, it is not theft when a person appropriates property belonging to another in the honest, though mistaken, belief that it is his. This applies whether he mistook the property for his own or whether, due to a mistaken belief regarding the civil law concerning the transfer of ownership, he honestly thought the property was now his: these are both mistakes of fact. However, it would not be a defence to argue that he honestly, though mistakenly, believed it was not against the law to appropriate someone else's property: this is a mistake of law.

In all cases the mistake must be an *honest* one. In some cases it must also be *reasonable*. The present position on this point was established in *R v. Williams* (1987):

(a) where the *mens rea* of the offence is either intention or 'Cunningham' recklessness, the mistake ned only be honest. There is no requirement that it also be reasonable, though the less reasonable the mistake, the less likely a jury is to believe it was honestly made.

(b) where the *mens rea* of the offence is either 'Caldwell' recklessness or negligence, the mistake must be both honest and reasonable. The law will not invest the reasonable person with the accused's unreasonable mistake.

(c) where the offence is one of strict liability (see below), mistake is no defence, even where it is both honest and reasonable.

Mistake is no defence where it results from voluntary intoxication (*R v. O'Grady* (1987)).

Intoxication

Whether intoxication (by drink or drugs) should be a defence raises a dilemma between policy and principle. As a matter of policy, it is wrong that an intoxicated offender should be able to avoid responsibility for their actions simply because of their intoxication. As a matter of principle, however, there can be no doubt that intoxication can prevent someone forming the required *mens rea*. In an attempt to resolve this dilemma, the law has developed principles based partly on the distinction between voluntary and involuntary intoxication, and partly upon the type of offence committed.

Involuntary intoxication: this is where the person is either forced to consume the intoxicating substance against their will, or where they consume it in complete ignorance of its intoxicating properties (for example, where a soft drink has been 'spiked' with alcohol). Intoxication is *not* involuntary where a person voluntarily consumes a substance, knowing it to be intoxicating, but being mistaken as to its strength (*R v. Allen* (1988)).

Involuntary intoxication is a defence to any crime where, taking his intoxicated state into account, the accused did not form the required *mens rea* (*R v. Sheehan* (1975); *R v. Pordage* (1975)).

Voluntary intoxication: this is where a person voluntarily consumes a substance, knowing it to be intoxicating. While (as might be expected) the law shows less sympathy for the voluntarily intoxicated offender, this may still be a defence where, taking his intoxicated state into account, he did not form the required *mens rea*.

Whether it will, in such circumstances, be allowed as a defence depends upon the type of offence committed. Voluntary intoxication may be a defence to crimes of *specific intent*, but not to crimes of *basic intent* (*DPP v. Majewski* (1976); *R v. Lipman* (1969)).

Crimes of specific intent:
- murder
- all attempts to commit a crime
- all offences where the *mens rea* extends beyond the *actus reus* (sometimes known as crimes of ulterior intent); for example, the *mens rea* of theft extends beyond the dishonesty of the appropriation because of the additional requirement of an intention to permanently deprive.

Crimes of basic intent:
● all other crimes, including manslaughter.

There are two further points regarding intoxication:

Dutch courage: voluntary intoxication will *not* be a defence to crimes of specific intent where the accused, having formed the intention to commit the crime, becomes intoxicated in order to overcome sober inhibitions (*i.e.* to acquire 'Dutch courage') which would otherwise prevent him from carrying out that intention (*Attorney General for Northern Ireland v. Gallagher* (1963)).

***Bona fide* medical treatment:** voluntary intoxication may be a defence to *any* crime where the intoxicating substance is consumed in pursuance of *bona fide* medical treatment or prescription. This applies where the effect of the substance is usually sedative or stabilising, provided the accused was not 'Cunningham' reckless in respect of a risk that the substance might induce aggressive, unpredictable or uncontrollable conduct (*R v. Bailey* (1983); *R v. Hardie* (1984)). The substance concerned does not have to have been medically prescribed.

Infancy

The position regarding the criminal capacity of minors is:

Children under ten years of age: are not criminally responsible for their actions (Children and Young Persons Act 1963, s.16). The law presumes that they are incapable of forming *mens rea*. However, the courts and local authorities do have powers outside the criminal law to deal with such children. Furthermore, where a child under ten commits an offence at the instigation of an adult, the adult may be liable through the innocent agency of the child.

Children between the ages of ten and fourteen: can only be convicted of a crime if it is proved that they had a 'mischievous discretion' (*C (a minor) v. DPP* (1995)). This means that in addition to proving both the *actus reus* and *mens rea*, it must be shown that the child knew that what they were doing was seriously wrong, rather than merely naughty (though it is not necessary to show they knew it was against the law).

Children over the age of fourteen: have full criminal responsibility. However, as might be expected, there are important differences in the approaches to the punishment of young and adult offenders.

Duress

A person may have a defence where they can show they were forced to commit the crime because of threats made to them by another person. This is known as acting under duress. For this defence to be successful, the accused must show:

(a) that he was (or may have been) forced to act as he did because, as a result of what he reasonably believed the threatener to have said or done, he had good reason to fear that if he did not act in this way, the threatener would kill him or cause him serious physical injury; and

(b) that a reasonable man, acting in the circumstances as the accused reasonably believed them to be and sharing those characteristics of the accused that would influence the effect of the threat upon him, would not have responded differently (*R v. Graham* (1982); *R v. Howe* (1986)).

This defence is also available where the threat of death or serious injury is aimed not at the accused himself, but at someone whom he is under a duty to protect. This obviously includes members of his family and may, in appropriate circumstances, include strangers; for example, where an armed robber threatens the life of a customer in order to force a bank cashier to hand over money.

Duress will *not* be a defence where:

(a) the accused had an opportunity before the commission of the offence to avoid the threatened consequences (*R v. Hudson and Taylor* (1971));

(b) the source of the threat is an organisation (for example, a criminal gang or terrorist group) which the accused joined

voluntarily and with the knowledge that threats of this kind might be made (*R v. Sharp* (1987));
(c) the offence concerned is murder (*R v. Howe* (1987)) or attempted murder (*R v. Gotts* (1992)).

Necessity

There is no general defence of necessity in the criminal law (*R v. Dudley and Stephens* (1884)). However, the courts have recognised a *limited* form of a necessity defence:

Duress of circumstances: this covers situations where the accused has been forced to act, not as a result of threats made by another person, but in response to the circumstances in which he finds himself (*R v.Conway* (1988); *R v. Martin* (1989)). Therefore, this defence is subject to the same two-part (subjective/objective) test and the same limitations as the defence of duress by threats (see above, p. 121).

Self-defence (and its variations)

Self-defence: where a person is faced with a violent, unlawful or indecent assault, he will be justified in using force to repel that assault. Both the decision to use force *and* the degree of force used must be (objectively) reasonable in the circumstances as he (subjectively) believed them to be (*R v. Wiliams* (1987); *R v. Owino* (1995)). In deciding the question of reasonableness regarding *both* issues, the following factors must be taken into account:
(a) the circumstances as the accused honestly believed them to be, even if this belief was mistaken (except where the mistake was due to voluntary intoxication—see above, p. 118).
(b) the time available to the accused to consider what to do (*Palmer v. R* (1971)).
Thus, a decision to use force or a degree of force used which may appear unreasonable with hindsight may be regarded as reasonable when the circumstances as the accused believed them to be and the time available for reflection are taken into account.
There is no requirement that the degree of force used be object-

ively proportionate to that threatened, or that the accused had sought to retreat or avoid the confrontation (*R v. Bird* (1985)). These are simply factors for the jury to take into account in deciding whether the accused's conduct was reasonable.

Defence of others/defence of property: these situations are governed by the same principles outlined above.

Acting in the prevention of crime: this is a statutory defence under the Criminal Law Act 1967. Section 3(1) provides:

> 'A person may use such force as is reasonable in the circumstances in the prevention of crime, or in effecting or assisting in the lawful arrest of offenders or suspected offenders or of persons unlawfully at large.'

This clearly has a considerable overlap with the defences outlined above and its application is governed by the same principles.

Consent of the victim

Generally, consent of the victim is no defence. However, there may be a defence to a charge of common assault where it is shown *both* that the victim consented *and* that the activity involved is not contrary to the public interest (*R v. Donovan* (1934); *R v. Brown* (1993)). Thus, consent may be a defence to a charge of common assault arising out of:

> 'properly conducted games and sports, lawful chastisement or correction, reasonable surgical interference, dangerous exhibitions, etc. These apparent exceptions can be justified as involving the exercise of a legal right, in the case of chastisement or correction, or as needed in the public interest, in the other cases.' (Attorney General's Reference (No. 6 of 1980 (1981), *per* Lord Lane C.J.).

Two aspects here require further explanation:

Surgical treatment: consent is necessarily a defence here to conduct which would otherwise amount to grievous bodily harm. Emergency surgical treatment without consent would appear to be justified either on grounds of public policy or necessity.

Sports: it would seem that players are held to have consented to contact incidental to the sport. This may include some instances of foul play, but *not* the deliberate (or 'professional') foul (*R v. Billingshurst* (1978)) or conduct which has nothing to do with the sport (for example, throwing a punch in a rugby scrum). The position of boxing is more unusual, in that the violent contact is not incidental to the sport but is rather its primary objective. However, it would seem that the same principles apply.

d. Strict liability in the criminal law

Offences of strict liabiilty are those for which there is no requirement of *mens rea* regarding one or more elements of the *actus reus*. For example, with possession of a prohibited substance, it is sufficient to show that the accused knew of the existence of the substance: it is not necessary to show that he knew what that substance was (*R v. Marriott* (1971)).

Almost all strict liability offences are created by statute. The courts have been reluctant to develop such offences at common law (blasphemous libel being one of the few examples) and employ a presumption of *mens rea* when interpreting criminal statutes. Thus, Parliament must use very clear words if it wishes to create an offence of this type.

The reason for this reluctance is clear: the imposition of strict liability is contrary to the general principles of the criminal law which, as has been seen, focus on the issue of fault and individual responsibility.

Lord Scarman (in *Gammon (Hong Kong) Ltd v. Attorney General of Hong Kong* (1984)) provided guidance for the identification of statutory offences of strict liability. He stated that:

(a) there is a presumption in favour of a requirement of *mens rea* when interpreting criminal statutes;

(b) the presumption is particularly strong where the offence is 'truly criminal';

(c) the presumption can only be displaced where the offence was clearly intended to be one of strict liability;

(d) this can only occur where the statute deals with an issue of social concern;

(e) even then, the presumption can only be displaced where the imposition of strict liability would encourage greater care to prevent the commission of the unlawful act.

Therefore, in identifying such offences, two main factors must be considered:

The wording of the statute: some words (such as 'use') are generally regarded as 'strict liability words', while others (such as 'knowingly') are generally regarded as *'mens rea* words'. However, there are no hard and fast rules here, and some words (such as 'cause' and 'permit') have been interpreted differently in different contexts.

The nature (or context) of the offence: given the above, this would seem to be the decisive factor. The courts have tended to draw a distinction between acts which are 'truly criminal' (for which *mens rea* is required) and acts which happen to be regulated by the criminal law (for which strict liability may be appropriate).

Therefore, it seems that strict liability offences fall into two categories:

The regulatory offence (or quasi-crime): for example, parking offences.

The public interest (or social danger) offence: for example, dangerous drugs, environmental pollution (*Alphacell Ltd v. Woodward* (1972)).

As strict liability represents a significant departure from general principle, it must be considered whether its use can be justified at all in the criminal law.

Arguments against: (a) it is contrary to general principle.

(b) it is objectionable and serves no useful purpose to punish someone who has taken reasonable care to comply with the law.

(c) it results in unnecessary social stigmatisation.

Arguments for: (a) while it may be generally desirable that criminal liability should depend upon proof of individual fault, there are circumstances where the collective or public interest in prohibition outweighs that individual interest.

(b) the imposition of strict liability may encourage positive steps to comply with the law, rather than merely negative action to avoid non-compliance.

(c) it avoids the complications that would otherwise arise in seeking to establish corporate liability for, for example, pollution offences.

(d) while fault (or the degree of fault) may not be relevant to liability, it would be taken into account in sentencing.

Also, while liability for such offences may be strict, it is *not* absolute. The accused may be able to raise one of the general defences outlined above. Furthermore, a statutory defence of due diligence or reasonable precautions is often provided, thereby making the offence, effectively, one of negligence liability.

Therefore, the use of strict liability in the criminal law may be justified in the limited and exceptional circumstances outlined above. However, its extensive use would be clearly unacceptable.

e. Vicarious and corporate liability in the criminal law

Vicarious liability: this is where one person is liable for the acts of another by virtue of the relationship between them. By far the most common and significant example of such a relationship is that between an employer and employee. This is a very important notion in the law of tort (see below, p. 162) but is clearly contrary to the central place given to individual fault or responsibility in criminal liability.

However, it may be argued that there is a limited role for vicarious liability even in the criminal law. For example, a lorry driver may be unaware that his lorry has faulty brakes until they actually fail. The 'real culprit' in such circumstances may well be his employer for failing to take steps to ensure that his vehicles are properly maintained. The possibility of vicarious liability may act to encourage employers to adopt good and safe working practices.

Vicarious criminal liability is sometimes expressly created by statute. In other instances it may be implied by the courts in giving statutory words an 'extended' meaning. For example, the word 'sell' may be interpreted to include not only the salesman himself but also the person employing him to do the selling. However, the courts may only do this in respect of strict liability offences: they will not attribute the *mens rea* of an employee to his employer (*Coppen v. Moore (No. 2)* (1898); *James & Sons Ltd v. Smee* (1955)). The one exception to this is the 'delegation principle' applied to licensees of licensed premises. Here the courts may attribute *mens rea*, but only where the licensee has delegated authority for at least part of the premises to an employee and is not present in that part at the time that the offence is committed.

There can be no vicarious liability for secondary participation in a crime (*i.e.* for aiding, abetting, counselling or procuring) (*Ferguson v. Weaving* (1951)) or for attempts to commit a crime (*Gardner v. Akeroyd* (1952)).

Corporate liability: corporations may become criminally liable in two ways:

    (a) they may be vicariously liable for the acts of their employees (see above);

    (b) through the doctrine of identification. Clearly a corporation does not have a mind of its own and, hence, cannot form *mens rea*. However, it may be held to have done so where an individual within the corporation who has sufficient authority to be regarded as its controlling mind (for example, a managing director) has, while engaged on corporation business, formed the required *mens rea*. For example, the corporation may be liable for fraud where a director dishonestly submits falsified VAT returns.

The Interpretation Act 1889 provides that the word 'person' includes corporations. Therefore, all statutory offences that refer to a 'person' can also, theoretically, be committed by a corporation. However, as a corporation cannot be imprisoned, it can only commit offences which are punishable by a fine (this includes manslaughter but not murder, which carries a mandatory sentence of imprisonment). Furthermore, there are other offences which, by their very nature, cannot be committed by a corporation (for example, bigamy, rape and incest).

The justification for corporate liability is unclear. The punishment falls not on the individual responsible (who may be convicted in his own right as a co-principal) but on the shareholders (and may ultimately fall on the consumer through higher prices). It is therefore questionable whether this additional liability is necessary. However, two related arguments may be advanced for its existence:

(a) it may (as with vicarious liability) act as an encouragement to good practice.

(b) it is sometimes necessary for effective stigmatisation and, hence, deterrence, as the corporation will wish to preserve its good name (which would remain untarnished if only the individual concerned were prosecuted).

f. The Law of Homicide

Homicide is simply the killing of another human being, and is not necessarily unlawful. Some killings are purely accidental while others may be justified. There are a number of forms of unlawful homicide:

- murder
- manslaughter
- causing death by dangerous driving
- child destruction
- infanticide
- genocide

The discussion here will focus on murder and manslaughter.

Murder

Murder is an offence at common law and is subject to a mandatory sentence of life imprisonment.

The *actus reus* of murder consists of:

(a) an unlawful act;

(b) which also causes the death of another human being.

The unlawful act is usually a direct assault on the victim's person, though this need not necessarily be the case. For example, in *R v. Hayward* (1908) it was held that causing death from fright alone was sufficient. Similarly, under the rules relating to causation discussed earlier, it could be murder where the victim, seeking to escape from a murderous assault, jumped from a window and died from the fall, *provided* the attempt to escape was reasonably foreseeable.

The victim must be a living human being: it is not possible to murder someone not yet born or already dead. Regarding birth, in order to be a victim of murder, the child must be wholly expelled from the mother's body and have an existence independent of the mother. Thus, where a child, having been born, dies as a result of injuries sustained in the womb, this may be murder. Where, however, the child is born dead as a result of those injuries, the appropriate offence would be child destruction. Where a child is killed during the first year of its life by its mother, the appropriate offence may be infanticide rather than murder. Regarding death, the courts adopt a test of brain death (*R v. Malcherek* (1981)).

Historically, for both murder and manslaughter, death had to occur within a year and a day of the injury being inflicted. This rule was originally introduced to resolve problems of causation. However, medical advances have removed this justification and the rule was abolished by the Law Reform (Year and a Day Rule) Act 1996. Nevertheless, the Attorney-General's consent is required for proceedings where the death occurs more than three years after the injury or where the person has already been convicted of an offence in circumstances connected with the death.

The *mens rea* of murder is traditionally referred to as *malice aforethought*. While this may be misleading (as neither ill-will nor premeditation are required), it is a vital concept as it is the presence of malice aforethought which distinguishes murder from manslaughter. There are two forms of malice aforethought (*R v. Moloney* (1985)):

    (a) an intention to kill (sometimes referred to as *express* malice);

    (b) an intention to cause grievous bodily harm (sometimes referred to as *implied* malice).

The test for intention is that outlined earlier in the general discussion of *mens rea*. Regarding implied malice, there is no need to show that the accused knew or foresaw any risk of death resulting from his actions. It is sufficient that he intended to cause grievous bodily harm and that death in fact resulted (*R v. Vickers* (1957)).

Manslaughter

There are two general categories of manslaughter: voluntary and involuntary.

Voluntary manslaughter
This refers to killings which would amount to murder (*i.e.* the accused has malice aforethought) but for the operation of one of three partial defences:

(a) diminished responsibility

(b) provocation

(c) killing in pursuance of a suicide pact
(Homicide Act 1957)

Involuntary manslaughter
This refers to killings without malice aforethought and takes one of two forms:

(a) constructive (or unlawful act) manslaughter

(b) gross negligence manslaughter
(*R v. Adomako* (1994))

Voluntary manslaughter

At common law there was only one form of voluntary manslaughter: killing under provocation. The Homicide Act 1957 gave statutory force to this category and added a further two: killing while suffering from diminished responsibility and killing in pursuance of a suicide pact.

Diminished responsibility (Homicide Act 1957, s.2): provides that it shall be voluntary manslaughter where a person kills another while 'suffering from such abnormality of mind (whether arising from a condition of arrested or retarded development of mind or any inherent causes or induced by disease or injury) as substantially impaired his mental responsibility for his acts or omission in doing ... the killing'.

Thus, in order to raise diminished responsibility, the accused must show:

(a) that he was suffering from an abnormality of mind (whether due to an internal or external cause);

(b) that this substantially impaired his mental responsibility for the killing.

A person's state of mind is abnormal if it is so different from that of ordinary people that a reasonable man would regard it as abnormal (*R v. Byrne* (1960)). This includes not only questions of perception and reason but also the ability to exercise will power. Thus, it may be diminished responsibility where a person, though they know it to be wrong, cannot control an irresistible impulse.

A 'substantial' impairment is one which is more than trivial but need not be total (*R v. Lloyd* (1967)).

This special defence clearly has similarities with both automatism and insanity and it is useful to contrast the differing requirements and effects of these 'mental state' defences:

	Defence to	Cause of	Degree of impairment required	Result
Automatism	All crimes	External	Total	Acquittal
Insanity	All crimes	Internal	Total	Special verdict
Diminished Responsibility	Murder only	Either	Substantial	Conviction for voluntary manslaughter

Provocation (Homicide Act 1957, s.3): provides that it is voluntary manslaughter where the killer was 'provoked (whether by things said or things done or by both together) to lose his self control' and that 'whether the provocation was enough to make a reasonable man do as he did shall be left to … the jury; and … the jury shall take into account everything both said and done according to the effect, in their opinion, it would have on a reasonable man'.

Thus, in order to raise provocation, the accused must show:

(a) that, as a result of things said or done or both together, he was provoked to lose his self control.

The loss of self control must be *sudden and temporary* (*R v. Duffy* (1949)). This requirement is intended to distinguish between genuinely uncontrollable reactions and calculated acts of revenge. However, it has caused a number of difficulties, particularly where women have delayed (albeit for a brief period) in striking back against abusive partners. However, it is now clear that this requirement does *not* mean that the response has to follow immediately upon the provocative conduct (*R v. Ahluwalia* (1992)). Furthermore, it is now recognised that any history of provocation *is* relevant in deciding whether the accused lost his self control: what might be termed 'last straw' provocation (*R v. Thornton* (1992)).

(b) that a reasonable man would, in those circumstances (including any history of provocation), have been provoked to lose his self control.

For this 'control' element, the reasonable man is someone with the self control expected of an ordinary person sharing the age and sex of the accused. Any other subjective characteristics of the accused which might result in his having a lesser degree of self control are *not* relevant (*DPP v. Camplin* (1978); *R v. Morhall* (1995)).

(c) that a reasonable man (having lost his self control) would (or may have) responded to the provocation in the same way as the accused.

For this 'response' element, the jury is entitled to consider the *entire factual situation* in which the accused found himself (*DPP v. Camplin* (1978); *R v. Morhall* (1995)). This includes, but is *not* limited to, the mental and physical characteristics of the accused. Thus, while a mental or physical characteristic of the accused is not relevant in deciding whether his loss of self control was reasonable, it may be relevant in deciding whether his subsequent conduct was reasonable. This is particularly so where the provocation was aimed at that characteristic (for example, where an impotent man is taunted about that condition).

Finally, the provocation need not come from the victim nor be aimed at the accused. It may still be a defence where the provocation comes from a third party (*R v. Davies* (1975)) or is aimed at a third party (*R v. Pearson* (1992)). It may still be raised even where the provocation is self-induced by the accused's own conduct (*R v. Johnson* (1989)). These are simply factors for the jury to consider in deciding whether the loss of self control and subsequent response were reasonable.

Suicide pacts (Homicide Act 1957, s.4): provides that it is voluntary manslaughter where one person kills another as part of a suicide pact between them. A suicide pact is defined as 'a common agreement between two or more persons having for its object the death of all of them, whether or not each is to take his own life' and that 'nothing done by a person who enters into a suicide pact shall be treated as done by him in pursuance of the pact unless it is done while he has the settled intention of dying in pursuance of the pact'.

Involuntary manslaughter

[handwritten: premeditated]

This is killing without malice aforethought and takes two forms (*R v. Adomako* (1994)):

Constructive (or unlawful act) manslaughter: the *actus reus* of this offence consists of:

  (a) an unlawful act

  (b) which is dangerous, in that it exposes others to the risk of some harm, albeit not serious harm (*R v. Church* (1965))

  (c) and which causes the death of the victim

The *mens rea* is that required for the unlawful act. It is not necessary to show that the accused knew the act was either unlawful or dangerous or that he was aware of the circumstances which make it dangerous. It is sufficient that a reasonable man would have been aware of those circumstances (*R v. Watson* (1989)) and would have regarded the act as dangerous (*DPP v. Newbury and Jones* (1976)).

Gross negligence manslaughter: the *actus reus* of this offence consists of:

  (a) a duty of care owed by the accused to the victim

  (b) a breach of that duty by the accused

  (c) that breach causing the death of the victim

The *mens rea* required is gross negligence which the jury considers justifies a criminal conviction. Lord Taylor C.J. stated in *R v. Prentice and others* (1993) that gross negligence could include:

  (a) indifference to an obvious risk of injury to health

  (b) actual foresight of the risk together with a decision to take it (essentially 'Cunningham' recklessness)

  (c) actual foresight of the risk together with an intention to avoid it but with a high degree of negligence in the attempt to avoid it

  (d) failure (going beyond mere inadvertence) to appreciate an obvious and serious risk (which appears to be similar to 'Caldwell' recklessness).

g. Non-fatal offences against the person

Common assault

Section 39 of the Criminal Justice Act 1988 provides that common assault and battery are summary offences punishable by up to six months' imprisonment and/or a fine. At common law, assault and battery were two separate offences and section 39 appears to preserve this distinction. However, section 40 refers only to common assault and in *R v. Lynsey* (1995) this was held to include both assault and battery. Thus it would seem that either assault or battery (in their common law senses) are now both to be regarded as 'common assault'. The elements of this offence must now be considered:

actus reus: either:

(a) *assault*: this is the placing of another in fear of immediate and unlawful personal violence. This may be done by acts alone (for example, raising one's fists at someone) or by acts and words together (for example, raising one's fists and saying 'I'm going to thump you!'). It is unclear whether words alone can amount to an assault, though they probably can. What is clear is that words can negate the effect of acts (for example, it would not be an assault to raise one's fists while saying 'If you were a younger man, I would thump you!') (*Tuberville v. Savage* (1669)): though this is not the case where the words merely announce a condition by which the victim can avoid the threatened violence (for example, raising one's fists while saying 'Unless you give me your money, I will thump you!' (*Blake v. Barnard* (1840))); or

(b) *battery*: this is the application of unlawful personal violence on another. Any degree of physical contact (however slight) without consent is sufficient. However, a person is held to have impliedly consented to everyday physical contact (for example, an accidental collision in a busy street, tapping on someone's shoulder to attract their attention). The application of force will usually be direct (for example, by hitting or spitting) but need not be so. For example, it would be a battery where A pulls B's chair away as B is sitting down. This example also emphasises that a battery does not have to be accompanied by an assault.

mens rea: either (*R v. Venna* (1976); *R v. Savage and Parmenter* (1991)):

(a) an intention to place another in fear of immediate and unlawful personal violence or 'Cunningham' (subjective) recklessness as to the risk of doing so; or

(b) an intention to apply unlawful personal violence to another or 'Cunningham' recklessness as to the risk of doing so.

More serious (or aggravated) assaults are provided for under the Offences Against the Person Act 1861:

Assault occasioning actual bodily harm

This is an offence under section 47 of the 1861 Act, punishable by imprisonment for up to five years. The elements of this offence are:

actus reus: it must be shown that the accused:

(a) committed a common assault

(b) which caused actual bodily harm

'Actual bodily harm' is harm which is more than trivial but which is not really serious (*DPP v. Smith* (1961)). This would indicate that the victim must be caused some noticeable discomfort, albeit of a minor and/or temporary nature. 'Harm' includes not only physical harm but also psychiatric harm (but not mere emotions, such as fear, distress or panic) (*R v. Chan-Fook* (1994)).

mens rea: it is sufficient to show the accused had either formed an intention or was 'Cunningham' reckless with regard to the assault and that actual bodily harm was in fact caused. It is *not* necessary to show that the accused either intended or foresaw that actual bodily harm would or might be caused (*R v. Savage and Parmenter* (1991)).

Unlawful and malicious wounding or infliction of grievous bodily harm

This is an offence under section 20 of the 1861 Act, punishable by imprisonment for up to five years. The elements of this offence are:

actus reus: either:
- (a) unlawful wounding. For wounding to occur, both the inner and outer skin must be broken (*Moriarty v. Brookes* (1834)); or
- (b) unlawful infliction of grievous bodily harm. 'Grievous bodily harm' means really serious bodily harm (*DPP v. Smith* (1961)).

Either of the above is sufficient: there may be a wounding without there also being grievous bodily harm, and *vice versa*.

mens rea: either (*R v. Savage and Parmenter* (1991)):
- (a) an intention to inflict some harm, albeit not serious harm; or
- (b) 'Cunningham' recklessness as to the infliction of some harm, albeit not serious harm.

It is *not* necessary to show that the accused intended or foresaw that wounding or really serious harm would or may result.

Unlawful and malicious wounding or causing grievous bodily harm with intent to do grievous bodily harm or resist lawful arrest

This is an offence under section 18 of the 1861 Act, punishable by up to life imprisonment. The elements of this offence are:

actus reus: as for section 20 (see above)

mens rea: either:
- (a) intention to do grievous bodily harm (recklessness is *not* sufficient); or
- (b)
  - (i) intention to resist lawful arrest; and
  - (ii) intention or 'Cunningham' recklessness as to the causing of some harm, albeit not serious harm.

2. CRIME AND PUNISHMENT

Introduction

There are two main reasons for the existence of a criminal justice system:

(a) there is a need for a mechanism to discourage antisocial conduct.

(b) there is a general moral sense that those who engage in such conduct deserve to be punished. Punishment is the correct moral result of criminal activity.

However, punishment, in that it involves the imposition of deprivation or suffering, is in itself an antisocial act. The most coherent justification put forward for its use is the 'social contract' theory developed in the eighteenth century by Enlightenment philosophers such as Beccaria. They argued that as part of the social bargain that forms the basis of society, individuals gave up the right to commit antisocial acts in return for society's protection from the antisocial acts of others. Therefore, society is justified in punishing those who, by committing crimes, break this bargain. This moved criminal theory away from the moral simplicity of the *lex talionis* (an eye for an eye), and towards a more rational, constructive and humane view of the aims of punishment.

The aims of punishment

Jeremy Bentham (in *An Introduction to the Principles of Morals and Legislation* (1780)) identified three main aims for the criminal justice system:

(a) to prevent all crime.

(b) to prevent the more serious crimes.

(c) to prevent re-offending.

It may be argued that any system seeking to achieve these aims will incorporate three elements:

Retribution: this is where the punishment is seen as the way in which society gains revenge on the criminal. It is based on the idea that the criminal deserves to be punished and that society gains a cathartic benefit from this. While the importance of the retributive element in punishment has been in decline, it can still be seen in the response to particularly horrifying crimes (for example, offences against children).

Deterrence: this is where the punishment is intended to discourage further crimes. Deterrence has two aspects:

(a) individual deterrence: it is hoped that the punishment will deter the individual criminal from re-offending;
(b) general deterrence: it is hoped that the punishment of the criminal will act as an example to deter others from committing crimes.

However, as many crimes are committed in the heat of the moment, while intoxicated or are opportunistic rather than considered, it would be wrong to over-emphasise punishment as a deterrent. Many offenders simply do not stop to consider the possible consequences of their actions. Others view the likelihood of being caught as so small that the risk is worth taking.

Rehabilitation: this is where the punishment is designed to discourage re-offending by rehabilitating the offender into the law-abiding mainstream of society, by reforming his character. It is based on the view that people are not born criminals but that they commit crimes for identifiable reasons. It follows that if the punishment regime addresses these reasons successfully, the criminal behaviour should stop.

Key concepts in effective punishment

Whichever balance is used of the three elements outlined above, there are four key concepts which must be incorporated into any successful criminal justice system:

Proportionality: the severity of the punishment should be proportionate to the gravity of the offence for three reasons:
(a) if the punishment is perceived as excessively harsh, there will be a reluctance to prosecute and convict. This creates the danger of the law falling into disrepute;
(b) without proportionality, there is no reason to commit minor rather than serious offences;
(c) without proportionality, there is nothing to deter the criminal from committing a further offence to avoid punishment for an earlier one.

Therefore, proportionality is essential to the element of deterrence and to maintain public confidence in the justice of the system. It is even implicit in the 'just desserts' policy of retribution.

Certainty: the more certain the prospect of punishment, the stronger the effect of its deterrent will be. The threat of even a very severe punishment is unlikely to deter if the chances of being caught are small. Therefore, it may be argued that investment in the police and other crime prevention strategies is likely to be more effective than investing in more prisons.

Publicity: informing people (through the education system and by other means) about the criminal justice system and the consequences of crime is vital to the success of the system. This again enhances the effect of the deterrent of punishment. People cannot be deterred by something they do not know.

Promptness: it is important that the system is efficient in the detection and punishment of crime. The more prompt the punishment, the clearer and more effective its association with the crime will be, both in the mind of the individual offender and in society at large.

The present approach to sentencing in the English courts

The present approach to sentencing by the English courts is governed by the Criminal Justice Act 1991 (as amended). Regarding adult offenders, the Act refers to three main forms of punishment;

Custodial sentences: the court can only pass a custodial sentence where either (s.1(2)):
  (a) the offence was so serious that only a custodial sentence can be justified; or
  (b) a custodial sentence is necessary to protect the public from serious harm.
In making this assessment, the court must take into account any aggravating or mitigating factors and any previous convictions.
  The court must also decide (except where the sentence is fixed by law; for example, for murder) upon the length of any custodial sentence. Section 2(2) provides that the length of the sentence shall be either:

(a) commensurate with the seriousness of the offence; or

(b) in the case of a violent or sexual offence, for such longer term as is necessary to protect the public from serious harm.

In *R v. Cunningham* (1992), Lord Taylor C.J. stated that 'the purpose of a custodial sentence must primarily be to punish and deter. Accordingly, the phrase 'commensurate with the seriousness of the offence' must mean commensurate with the punishment and deterrence which the seriousness of the offence requires'. This emphasises that the notions of deterrence and proportionality are central to the 1991 Act.

Community sentences: where a custodial sentence is not justified, the court may consider a community sentence (such as probation or a community service order). Again, a community sentence can only be passed where it is justified by the seriousness of the offence (s.6(1)) and any restriction on liberty involved must be commensurate with the seriousness of the offence (s.6(2)).

Fines: alternatively, or in addition to, the above sentences, the court may impose a fine. The amount of the fine must reflect the seriousness of the offence and must take into account the offender's financial circumstances (s.18).

The court may also order the offender to compensate the victim of the crime, and may in some cases (for example, drugs offences) confiscate any assets gained as a result of the crime.

Special rules apply to both young offenders (for example, detention in a Young Offenders' Institution rather than adult prison) and mentally ill offenders. Regarding mentally ill offenders, the court must obtain a medical report before sentencing and must take into account the likely effect of the sentence on the offender's illness and any treatment regime (s.4).

The effectiveness of the criminal justice system

Doubts have been expressed regarding the effectiveness of the present range of sanctions, particularly custodial sentences. Official statistics reveal that approximately two-thirds of male offenders are reconvicted within four years of release. It may be argued that this is due to weaknesses in rehabilitation programmes in frequently overcrowded prisons, and a lack of support following release. While community sentences are not significantly more successful in this respect, they are considerably cheaper to implement. Community sanctions also allow the offender to work and remain with their family. The financial and social costs of custody are in many cases not justified by its results.

It may also be argued that the present system pays too much attention to the consequences of crime, and not enough to its causes or prevention. While acknowledging that social and economic factors do not excuse criminal behaviour, the causative elements must be addressed if effective crime prevention strategies are to be developed. As Lord Scarman observed in his report on the Brixton disorders of 1981, 'the social conditions in Brixton do not provide an excuse for disorder. But the disorders cannot be fully understood unless they are seen in the context of complex political, social and economic factors which together create a predisposition towards violent protest' (Leslie Scarman, *The Scarman Report: The Brixton Disorders 10–12 April 1981*, Penguin, pp. 194–195).

Section Six: THE LAW OF TORT

Introduction

A tort is a civil wrong, other than a breach of trust or breach of contract. The law of tort, therefore, provides remedies for:
  (a) the intentional and direct interference with another's person, property or land (**trespass**);
  (b) the indirect interference with another's land (**nuisance**);
  (c) the unintentional and careless interference with another's person or property (**negligence**);
  (d) the slighting of another's reputation (**defamation**).
It also protects various more specialised interests (such as business and economic interests), and has specific rules relating to liability for premises and animals.

Prior to examining some of these torts in more detail, it is useful to contrast tortious, criminal and contractual liability:

	Criminal	Contract	Tort
Nature of obligations	mandatory	voluntary	mandatory
Responsibility for enforcement	state	individual	individual

Thus, the criminal law consists of general (or public) obligations, binding on all citizens, and enforced by the state. In contrast, the law of contract consists of private obligations, voluntarily entered into, and enforced by the individuals concerned. The law of tort is a rather curious hybrid, consisting of general (or public obligations), binding on all citizens, but which are left to individuals to enforce.

a. Negligence

Negligence may be defined as a failure to take reasonable care where a duty to do so exists, and where that failure causes recoverable loss or damage to the person to whom the duty is owed.

Therefore, negligence is a more precise concept than simple carelessness, and is only actionable upon proof of damage.

Negligence gradually emerged as a distinct tort from the tort of trespass. Its separate existence was established conclusively by the House of Lords in *Donoghue v. Stevenson* (1932). Here, for the first time, the House of Lords sought to identify the general principles underlying the tort of negligence, and Lord Atkin advanced his famous *neighbour principle*:

(a) you are under a duty to take reasonable care to avoid acts or omissions which you can reasonably foresee might injure your neighbour;

(b) your neighbour is someone so closely and directly affected by your actions that you ought reasonably to have them in mind as being so affected when considering those actions.

These notions of a duty of care and neighbourhood remain the central foundations of the modern tort of negligence. Following various refinements and variations since 1932, it would now appear that five requirements must be met for negligence liability to arise:

(a) the damage suffered by the plaintiff must disclose **a cause of action**;

(b) the defendant must have owed the plaintiff a **duty of care**;

(c) the defendant must have been in **breach** of that duty;

(d) the breach of duty must have been a **cause in fact** of the plaintiff's damage;

(e) the plaintiff's damage must have been a **reasonably fore-seeable consequence** of the defendant's breach of duty.

The cause of action

The forms of damage which are recoverable in negligence are:

(a) personal injury;

(b) physical damage to property;

(c) economic loss *consequential on* either (a) or (b).

However, pure economic loss is generally not recoverable (*Spartan Steel & Alloys Ltd v. Martin & Co (Contractors) Ltd* (1973); *D & F Estates Ltd v. Church Commissioners* (1989); *Murphy v. Brentwood District Council* (1990)). This limitation is not a matter of principle (as pure economic loss is often reasonably foreseeable). Rather, it is a matter of policy to avoid placing the defendant in a position of almost unlimited liability.

There is one important exception to this general position regarding pure economic loss. Pure economic loss *is* recoverable where there is a *special relationship* between plaintiff and defendant; *i.e.* where the plaintiff was relying on the specialist skill and knowledge of the defendant (*Hedley Byrne & Co Ltd v. Heller & Partners Ltd* (1964); *Junior Books Ltd v. Veitchi Co Ltd* (1982); *Simaan General Contracting Co v. Pilkington Glass Ltd (No. 2)* (1988)).

The duty of care

As noted above, Lord Atkin's original formulation of neighbourhood as the test for duty of care has been subject to a number of refinements (see, for example, *Anns v. Merton London Borough Council* (1978); *Yuen Kun Yeu v. Attorney General of Hong Kong* (1988)).

The present test is one of *proximity*, *i.e.* there must be a sufficiently proximate (or close) relationship between plaintiff and defendant so that it is just and reasonable in the circumstances to impose on the defendant a duty of care towards the plaintiff (*Caparo Industries plc v. Dickman* (1990); *Davis v. Radcliffe* (1990)). For proximity to arise, there must be neighbourhood (in the sense of foreseeability of harm). However, neighbourhood alone does not automatically amount to proximity. The court must also consider previous cases by way of analogy and, where appropriate (see, for example, *Hill v. Chief Constable of West Yorkshire* (1988)), questions of public policy.

Therefore, proximity is a more flexible (and less predictable) notion than that of neighbourhood.

There are two particular situations where the courts have imposed additional requirements (over and above mere neighbourhood) in order to satisfy the requirement of proximity and, hence, to give rise to a duty of care:

(a) **negligent statements:** in *Hedley Byrne & Co Ltd v. Heller & Partners Ltd* (1964), the House of Lords held that liability for negligent statements must be treated differently (and in a more restricted way) from liability for negligent acts because:
    (i) reasonably careful people tend to be more careful over what they do than what they say;
    (ii) while negligent acts tend to have a limited range of effect (giving rise to a limited amount of liability), negligent words can have a much wider effect (for example,

where they are broadcast) and could give rise to excessive and almost unlimited liability;

(iii) negligent words generally cause only pure economic loss which again, as noted above, could involve the defendant in excessive liability.

Therefore, rather than a mere relationship of neighbourhood, a *special relationship* is required to give rise to the necessary proximity in such cases. According to *Caparo Industries plc v. Dickman* (1990), a special relationship arises where:

(a) the person seeking the information or advice was relying on the other to exercise care and skill in their reply;

(b) such reliance was reasonable in the circumstances;

(c) the maker of the statement knew that his statement would be communicated to the inquirer (either as an individual or member of an identifiable class) specifically in connection with a particular transaction or transactions of a particular kind;

(d) the maker of the statement knew that the inquirer would be very likely to rely on it for the purpose of deciding whether or not to enter into that transaction or transactions of that kind.

There is *no* requirement that the maker of the statement be in the business of giving information or advice of the type sought. It is sufficient that he holds himself out as possessing the required skill or knowledge and that the inquirer reasonably relies on this (*Chaudhry v. Prabhakar* (1988)).

(b) nervous shock: nervous shock is a precise term meaning a recognised psychiatric illness (for example, pathological grief, Post-Traumatic Stress Disorder) caused by shock. The law does *not* recognise claims for ordinary grief or sorrow, no matter how deeply felt.

As with negligent statements, it is the potential breadth of liability which is the prompt for limitations here. As Lord Wilberforce observed in *McLoughlin v. O'Brian* (1982), 'just because 'shock' in its nature is capable of affecting so wide a range of people ... [there is] ... a very real need for the law to place some limitation on the extent of admissible claims'.

Therefore, it would seem that a person is owed a duty of care in respect of nervous shock where:

(a) the shock is consequent upon physical injury to himself; or

(b) the shock is consequent upon a reasonably apprehended fear
     of physical injury to himself, even though no injury in fact
     occurs (*Dulieu v. White* (1901)); and

(c) personal injury (whether physical or psychological) to the
     plaintiff is reasonably foreseeable (*Page v. Smith* (1995)).

The position is a little more complicated where the shock is caused
by injury or fear of injury to another. The House of Lords stated
the present position here when considering a series of test cases
arising from the Hillsborough Stadium disaster (*Alcock and others v.
Chief Constable of South Yorkshire Police* (1991)): a person is owed a
duty of care in respect of nervous shock where:

(a) the shock is consequent upon physical injury to another and:

   (i) the plaintiff sees or hears (or some equivalent thereof)
        the accident itself or its immediate aftermath; and

  (ii) the plaintiff (the secondary victim) has a close relation-
        ship of love and affection with the injured person (the
        primary victim) (*McFarlane v. E E Caledonia Ltd*
        (1993)); or

 (iii) the plaintiff is a rescuer (*Chadwick v. British Transport
        Commission* (1967)); and

  (iv) psychological injury to the plaintiff (the secondary
        victim) is reasonably foreseeable (*Page v. Smith* (1995)).

(b) the shock is consequent upon a reasonably apprehended fear
     of physical injury to another, even though no injury in fact
     occurs, and the requirements stated in (i) and (ii) or (iii)
     above are met.

The 'immediate aftermath' of the accident extends to the hospital
to which the injured person is taken and persists for as long as
that person remains in the state produced by the accident, up to
and including immediate post-accident treatment.

The breach of duty

The defendant will be in breach of his duty of care if he fails to
show reasonable care. This is essentially an *objective* test, measuring
the defendant's conduct against the degree of care a reasonable
man would have exercised in the same circumstances.

(a) **the reasonable man:** the reasonable man is expected to
     possess a certain amount of basic knowledge (for example, that

acid burns) and to show a basic or ordinary level of skill. Generally, expert skill or knowledge is not expected unless the defendant has claimed such knowledge or skill (*Phillips v. William Whiteley Ltd* (1938)). Even where expert skill or knowledge is required, the standard expected remains that of the *reasonably competent* expert in the given field.

It may be evidence of the fact that the defendant has acted reasonably to show that he acted in accordance with general, accepted or approved practice in the given field. Any such comparison must be with the accepted practice at the material time, discounting any subsequent developments, alterations or advances (*Roe v. Minister of Health* (1954)). However, such a comparison will not help the defendant where it would have been clear to a reasonable man that the accepted practice was itself negligent (*Cavanagh v. Ulster Weaving Co Ltd* (1960)).

An exclusively objective test would, in some circumstances, lead to injustice. Therefore, there are circumstances where the court will modify the objective standard by taking into account certain subjective characteristics of the defendant:

(a) mental or physical incapacity may make it impossible for the defendant to show reasonable care. It would be unjust to hold them negligent in failing to show a degree of care it is impossible for them to achieve. However, such a person may be negligent in placing themselves in a position which requires them to exercise a degree of care they know they are unable to achieve.

(b) young children are not required to show the same degree of care as adults. An allowance is made as their youth and immaturity may prevent them appreciating fully the risks and consequences of their actions (*Gough v. Thorne* (1966)).

(c) the elderly are not expected to show the same degree of physical or mental agility or speed of reflex as that of a younger adult (*Daly v. Liverpool Corporation* (1939)). The allowance made here is less than that for children, as the elderly clearly have the benefit of knowledge and experience which the child does not. The law also requires people to take account of the effects of ageing and a failure to do so may itself amount to negligence.

(d) the court may take account of illness on the part of the defendant *provided* it is both sudden and incapacitating and there has been no forewarning (*Ryan v. Youngs* (1938)).

(b) **reasonable care:** in deciding what degree of care amounts
to reasonable care in the circumstances, the courts will consider two main factors:
   (i) the degree of risk created by the defendant's conduct.
        This may be so slight that the reasonable man would be
        entitled to ignore it (*Bolton v. Stone* (1951)). Therefore,
        the general approach is that the greater the degree of
        risk created, the greater the degree of care that should
        be taken to guard against it.
   (ii) the seriousness of the potential harm. Again, the greater
        the potential harm, the greater the obligation to take
        care to prevent it (*Paris v. Stepney Borough Council* (1951)).
The court may also take into account the social utility of the
defendant's activities and the cost and practicability of taking precautions against the risk.

(c) **proof of breach:** the burden of proving breach lies with the
plaintiff. This burden is the civil burden of showing that, on
the balance of probabilities, the defendant was in breach of
duty.
   However, for a variety of practical reasons, it may be extremely
difficult (or even impossible) for the plaintiff to present definite
proof of the defendant's breach. In such circumstances, the plaintiff
may be able to rely on the *res ipsa loquitor* maxim. This is a rule of
evidence which asks the court to accept that 'the facts speak for
themselves' and to infer a breach of duty from the general circumstances of the case. For the maxim to apply, two requirements must
be met (*Scott v. London & St Katherine Docks Co* (1865)):
   (i) the accident must be of a type that does not normally
        occur without someone having been negligent;
   (ii) the circumstances must not merely indicate negligence
        by someone but negligence on the part of the defendant.
The maxim can only be used to establish breach of duty. It cannot
be relied on to establish the required causal link between the
defendant's breach of duty and the plaintiff's damage.

The causal link

For the defendant to be liable, there must be a clear, unbroken
causal link between his breach of duty and the damage suffered by

the plaintiff, *i.e.* the breach must be a cause in fact of the damage. This is established by the application of the *but for* test; *i.e.* but for the defendant's breach of duty, would the damage to the plaintiff have occurred? Where, on the balance of probabilities, the damage would not have occurred, then the defendant will be held responsible. Where, by contrast, the damage would probably have occurred in any event, the defendant will not be liable (*Barnett v. Chelsea & Kensington Hospital Management Committee* (1969); *Hotson v. East Berkshire Health Authority* (1987); *Wilsher v. Essex Area Health Authority* (1988)).

The defendant's breach need not be the sole cause of the damage. It is sufficient that it made a *significant material contribution* (*Bonningtons Castings Ltd v. Wardlaw* (1956)). However, it must have been a cause of the damage: merely increasing the risk of damage is not sufficient (*Wilsher v. Essex Area Health Authority* (1988); *Page v. Smith (No. 2)* (1996)).

Foreseeability of harm and remoteness of damage

In addition to establishing a factual causal link, the plaintiff must also establish that the breach was a cause in law of the damage for liability to arise. Following the decision of the Privy Council in *The Wagon Mound (No. 1)* (1961), the defendant will only be liable for damage which is a *reasonably foreseeable consequence* of his breach of duty. Damage which is not reasonably foreseeable is regarded as *too remote* from the breach and, therefore, not recoverable.

In establishing that the damage was reasonably foreseeable, the plaintiff does not have to show that the *precise* nature, extent or manner of occurrence was foreseeable (*Stewart v. West African Air Terminals Ltd* (1964)). What must be established is that the damage suffered was a reasonably foreseeable *type* of damage, occurring in a reasonably foreseeable *manner*. For example, in *Hughes v. Lord Advocate* (1963), burns sustained in a gas explosion (which was itself unforeseeable) were held to be within the general range of injuries which might reasonably foreseeably arise from leaving a paraffin lamp unattended at roadworks. In *Bradford v. Robinson Rentals Ltd* (1967), frostbite (though itself unforeseeable) was held to be within the general range of reasonably foreseeable injuries resulting from exposure to cold. However, in *Doughty v. Turner Manufacturing Co Ltd* (1964), injuries sustained when an asbestos cover fell into a vat of chemicals, causing them to erupt, were held to be outside the general range (and therefore unforeseeable) of reasonably foreseeable injuries which might result from being splashed by the chemicals: while splashing was reasonably foreseeable, the chemical eruption was not. Therefore, it is sometimes difficult to predict when the courts will regard unusual injuries or manners of occurrence as being unforeseeable or as being merely an unusual variation of reasonably foreseeable consequences.

There is no requirement that the extent of the damage be reasonably foreseeable (*Vacwell Engineering Co Ltd v. BDH Chemicals Ltd* (1971)). This principle stands alongside the *thin skull* rule, which requires that the defendant take his victim as he finds him. Therefore, the defendant cannot argue that he is not responsible for damage aggravated by the physical (*Dulieu v. White* (1901)) or mental (*Brice v. Brown* (1984)) peculiarities of the plaintiff. That this rule survives the decision in *The Wagon Mound* is clear from the decision in *Smith v. Leech Brain & Co Ltd* (1962), where a latent cancer was triggered into activity by a burn.

Defences to negligence

Where the plaintiff has met the five requirements explained above, the defendant will be liable unless he is able to rely on a defence. There are three main possibilities here:

(a) **contributory negligence:** this is where the plaintiff's damage is due, in part, to his own negligence. Under the Law Reform (Contributory Negligence) Act 1945, this is a *partial* defence, allowing the court to apportion responsibility for the damage between the plaintiff and defendant and reduce the defendant's liability accordingly. The defendant must show:
  (i) that the plaintiff failed to exercise reasonable care for his own safety (*Davies v. Swan Motor Co (Swansea) Ltd* (1949)).
  (ii) that this failure made a material contribution to the plaintiff's damage (*Jones v. Livox Quarries Ltd* (1952)).
In apportioning responsibility, the court will take two factors into account:
  (a) the extent to which the actions of the plaintiff and defendant were a cause of the damage (the *causative potency* test).

(b) the degree to which the plaintiff and defendant departed from the standards of the reasonable man (the *degree of blameworthiness* test).

For example, failure to wear a seat belt will generally result in a reduction of 25 per cent where wearing the belt would have eliminated the injury completely, and 15 per cent where the injury would have been less severe (*Froom v. Butcher* (1976)).

As with the position of the defendant in general negligence, the court may modify the test of reasonableness by taking into account certain subjective characteristics of the plaintiff. Regarding contributory negligence, in addition to the factors of mental or physical incapacity, youth or old age, the court may also take into account the following:

(a) where contributory negligence is alleged against a worker, consideration may be given to the fact that the worker's appreciation of risk may have been lessened through familiarity with the work or through the noise and stress of the workplace (*Grant v. Sun Shipping Co Ltd* (1948)).

(b) where the plaintiff has been placed in a position of danger by the defendant's negligence and, in the agony of the moment, seeks to escape this danger, he will not be contributory negligent should this decision turn out to be mistaken (*Jones v. Boyce* (1816)), *provided* his apprehension of danger is reasonable. This remains so even where the plaintiff has time to reflect upon his situation (*Haynes v. Harwood* (1935)). However, while the plaintiff may not be contributory negligent in his decision to attempt to escape, he may be negligent in his choice of method or its operation (*Sayers v. Harlow UDC* (1958)).

(b) **volenti non fit injuria**: *volenti* (consent to the risk) is a *complete* defence to negligence. However, the circumstances in which it may be raised are severely limited and it is of little practical application today. This is partly because the courts prefer to find a plaintiff contributory negligent (allowing them to apportion responsibility) rather than as being *volens* to the risk. For example, a plaintiff who accepts a lift from a driver he knows has been drinking will generally be regarded as contributory negligent (*Owens v. Brimmell* (1977)). However, *volenti* may apply where the plaintiff is aware that the driver is so drunk that an accident is a virtual certainty (*Ashton v. Turner* (1981); *Morris v. Murray* (1990)). Furthermore, the effectiveness of consent to express exclusions of liability has been significantly restricted by the Unfair Contract Terms Act 1977 (see below).

Nevertheless, *volenti* may be inferred from the plaintiff's conduct where four requirements are met (*ICI Ltd v. Shatwell* (1965)):

(a) the plaintiff must have been aware of the defendant's negligent conduct;

(b) the plaintiff must have been aware of the risk to himself that this created;

(c) the plaintiff must have continued to participate freely in the activity in the face of this knowledge;

(d) the damage suffered must have been a reasonably foreseeable consequence of the risk consented to.

The position of rescuers: *volenti* cannot be raised against a rescuer *provided* the decision to attempt a rescue was a reasonable one (*Haynes v. Harwood* (1935); *Cutler v. United Dairies (London) Ltd* (1933)). This remains so even where the rescuer knows there is a virtual certainty of injury. Furthermore, even where the decision to rescue was unreasonable, or where the rescuer has been negligent in his choice of method or its operation, the courts will generally regard this as contributory negligence rather than *volenti*. This preferential treatment is due to the fact that the courts do not wish to discourage people from acting as rescuers.

The courts do not make any fundamental distinction here between the layman and the professional rescuer (*Ogwo v. Taylor* (1987)). The fact that a person's employment is inherently dangerous does not make them *volens* to a risk arising from another's negligence. However, the particular skills and knowledge of the professional are a relevant consideration in deciding whether someone has exercised reasonable care for their own safety for the purposes of assessing contributory negligence.

(c) exclusion of liability: the defendant may seek to rely on an undertaking by the plaintiff to accept the risk of negligence in order to exclude or limit his liability. However, as noted above, the extent to which he can do this is limited by the Unfair Contract Terms Act 1977:

(a) Section 2(1) provides that a person cannot, by reference to any contractual term or non-contractual notice, exclude or restrict *business* liability for causing death or personal injury through negligence.

(b) Section 2(2) provides that such liability for other forms of loss or damage can only be excluded or restricted in so far as the term or notice is reasonable;

(c) Section 2(3) provides that a person's agreement to or awareness of such a term or notice does not, in itself, amount to *volenti*.

Nevertheless, there may still be certain non-business situations where such undertaking would be effective in excluding or restricting the defendant's liability.

b. Occupiers' Liability

One area where the law has identified a particular duty owed to others is that of the duty owed by occupiers to those who visit their premises. This is governed by the provisions of the Occupiers' Liability Acts 1957 and 1984:

The Occupiers' Liability Act 1957

This Act concerns the duty owed by an occupier to lawful visitors:

(a) **the common duty of care:** under section 2, the occupier owes a common duty of care to all lawful visitors to his premises. This is a duty to take reasonable care to ensure the visitor is reasonably safe when using the premises for all the purposes for which he is invited or permitted to be there. This applies to the visitor's physical safety in all circumstances but only to his property in respect of damage caused by structural defects in the premises (s.1).

What amounts to reasonable care is governed by the same principles as the general tort of negligence (see above, p. 148). However, the Act does make specific provision for two particular categories of visitor:

(i) *children*: a higher degree of care should be shown to child visitors. In particular, the occupier must take special care in respect of any allurements on the premises (*Glasgow*

Corporation v. Taylor (1922)). An allurement is something tempting or attractive to children but which is also potentially dangerous (for example; bonfires, berries, building materials, railway trucks).

(ii) *professionals*: a lower degree of care may be shown to visiting professionals or specialists in respect of risks or hazards incidental to their calling or profession (*Roles v. Nathan* (1963)).

(b) **lawful visitors:** there are four main categories of lawful visitor:

(i) *invitees*: an invitee is someone permitted to enter the premises by the occupier and whose presence is in the interests of the occupier (for example, customers in a shop or pub, guests at a party).

(ii) *licensees*: a licensee is someone permitted to enter the premises by the occupier but whose presence is of no interest to the occupier (for example, children recovering a lost ball).

(iii) *contractual visitors*: a contractual visitor is someone permitted to enter the premises under a contract with the occupier (for example, a window cleaner or milkman).

(iv) *statutory visitors*: a statutory visitor is someone with statutory authority to enter the premises (for example, a police officer or postman).

The common duty of care is not owed to common law visitors, other than invitees and licensees (*Greenhalgh v. British Railways Board* (1969)). A common law visitor is someone entitled to enter the premises by reason of some private or public right, such as a right of way. However, the occupier is under a common law duty not to do anything positive which might make their entry dangerous. They may also be protected under the 1984 Act. Also, the common duty is not owed to trespassers, though they are owed a common law duty of humanity (*British Railways Board v. Herrington* (1972)) and may also be protected under the 1984 Act.

(c) **the occupier:** an occupier is anyone who is in control of the premises (*Wheat v. E Lacon & Co Ltd* (1966)). There is no requirement that the occupier have any legal or equitable interest in the premises, nor need they be in exclusive possession of the premises. For example, both a building owner and a building contractor may be occupiers for the purposes of the Act.

(d) **premises:** 'premises' includes not only land and buildings, but also any fixed or movable structure, including any vehicle, vessel and aircraft. Thus, the provisions of the Act have been held to apply to ships, cranes, scaffolding, ladders, piers and sea platforms.

(e) **exclusion of liability:** the occupier can modify, restrict or exclude his liability under the Act by agreement or otherwise. However, the possibility of excluding or restricting *business* liability for negligence (which includes breach of the common duty under the Act) is severely constrained by the Unfair Contract Terms Act 1977 (see above p. 152).

(f) **defences:** there are three main defences available:
    (i) contributory negligence (see above p. 150);
    (ii) warnings: where the occupier has given a clear warning of danger which, if observed, would make the visitor safe, the occupier will not be liable for damage caused by the visitor's failure to observe the warning. Whether the warning is effective depends in part on the nature of the warning itself and in part upon the likely nature of potential visitors. A warning which would be effective against an adult visitor may not be effective against a child visitor.
    (iii) *volenti*: this may arise where the visitor was fully aware of the danger or risk on the premises, knew of the risk to himself this created and continued to remain on the premises in the face of that knowledge.

The Occupers' Liability Act 1984

This Act concerns the duty owed by an occupier to visitors other than lawful visitors (as defined for the purposes of the 1957 Act):

(a) **the limited duty:** unlike the general duty owed to lawful visitors under the 1957 Act, the 1984 Act imposes only a limited duty. This is a duty to take reasonable care to ensure the visitor is not injured as a result of *specific dangers* on the premises. A danger is a specific danger where:

  (a) the occupier is aware of the danger or has reasonable grounds to believe it exists.

  (b) the occupier knows or has reasonable grounds to believe that the other person is in the vicinity of the danger or is likely to come into the vicinity.

  (c) the danger is one against which, under all circumstances, the occupier may reasonably be expected to offer the other person protection. Here, the purpose for the other person being on the premises clearly affects whether he ought reasonably to be offered protection. For example, a burglar would receive less consideration than a child who had strayed onto the premises.

The limited duty only protects the visitor's physical safety. It offers no protection to his property.

(b) **the occupier, premises and defences:** the same principles and definitions apply as for the 1957 Act.

(c) **implied licensees:** a trespasser may become an implied licensee in circumstances where the occupier is aware of their presence and does nothing to prevent or discourage it nor expressly forbids it (for example, children who regularly gain access to the premises to play or take a short cut; *Edwards v. British Railway Executive* (1952)). In such circumstances, the visitor would then be owed the common duty under the 1957 Act.

c. Nuisance

The tort of nuisance has three distinct forms:

Private nuisance

Private nuisance is the indirect and unreasonable interference with the use or enjoyment of neighbouring land (*Sedleigh-Denfield v. O'Callaghan* (1940)).

A nuisance may be caused by many different things, common causes being noise, smoke, odours, fumes, water and plant and tree roots.

The basis of liability here is the failure to meet the reasonable expectations of one's neighbours. While this has clear similarities with negligence, there are also important differences. In negligence, the question is whether the defendant's conduct was reasonable, while in nuisance the question is whether the effect of that conduct on the defendants neighbours is reasonable. Therefore, if the defendant's conduct in fact causes an actionable nuisance, it is no defence to show that he has taken reasonable care to prevent this. If the defendant cannot carry on a particular activity without causing an actionable nuisance, then he should not continue with that activity or, at least, should continue it somewhere else (*Rapier v. London Tramways Co* (1893)). This means that nuisance can, in certain circumstances, take on the appearance of a tort of strict liability.

(a) **proof of damage—the essential element:** a nuisance is only actionable where it causes damage to the plaintiff's interests. This requirement is clearly satisfied where the nuisance causes physical damage to the plaintiff's land, as this is always unreasonable. Where the damage complained of is disturbance to the use of enjoyment, this must be more than trivial (*Andreae v. Selfridge* (1938)): the law expects a degree of give-and-take between neighbours (*Bamford v. Turnley* (1862)).

(b) **other relevant factors:** while proof of damage is essential to a successful nuisance action, there are a number of other factors which the court may consider:
   (i) generally, the nuisance must be of a continuing or regular nature. Isolated or irregular instances will not normally amount to a nuisance (*Bolton v. Stone* (1951)). However, where the defendant is responsible for a continuous state of affairs with the potential for nuisance, he may be liable immediately should a nuisance in fact occur (*Spicer v. Smee* (1946)).
   (ii) where the damage complained of is disturbance to use or enjoyment, the court may consider the character of the neighbourhood (*St Helen's Smelting Co v. Tipping* (1865)). What may be reasonable in an industrial area

may not be so in a residential area. Similarly, what may be reasonable in a busy city may not be so in a quiet country village.

(iii) the fact that the plaintiff may be unusually sensitive is *not* relevant to the issue of liability: the test remains the expectations of the reasonable neighbour (*Robinson v. Kilvert* (1889)). However, once liability has been established, any unusual sensitivity may be relevant to the question of remedies (*McKinnon Industries Ltd v. Walker* (1951)).

(iv) while malice on the part of the defendant is not an essential requirement, the presence of malice may tip the balance, converting otherwise reasonable conduct into an actionable nuisance (*Christie v. Davey* (1893); *Hollywood Silver Fox Farm Ltd v. Emmett* (1936)).

(v) the defendant may be liable for a nuisance caused by the fault of another or due to natural causes. This is known as 'adoption' or 'continuance' of nuisance, and arises where the defendant knew or ought to have known of the nuisance and failed to take reasonable steps to stop it (*Leakey v. National Trust* (1980)).

(c) **the plaintiff:** the plaintiff must have a legal or equitable interest in the land affected (*Malone v. Laskey* (1907)). Where the damage complained of is disturbance to use or enjoyment, the plaintiff must also be in actual possession (occupation) of the land (*Cooper v. Crabree* (1882)). However, where the damage is physical damage, a person with an interest out of possession (for example, a landlord) may sue (*Colwell v. St Pancras Borough Council* (1904)).

(d) **the defendant:** an action for private nuisance may be brought against the occupier of the offending land, the creator of the nuisance or any person authorising the nuisance (for example, a landlord).

(e) **defences:** there are three main defences available:

(i) consent of the plaintiff: where the plaintiff has expressly consented to the nuisance, this will be a defence *provided* it is true consent; *i.e.* to both the nature and extent of the nuisance.

(ii) prescription: this is a form of implied consent. Where the defendant has been committing the nuisance for more than twenty years and has done so without force, secrecy or permission (*nec vi, nec clam, nec precario*), this will be a defence against a plaintiff who has not complained during this time. However, this defence is of little practical application today as the time starts running from the time the particular plaintiff became aware of the nuisance (*Sturges v. Bridgman* (1879)). Therefore, it is no defence to argue that the plaintiff 'came into' the nuisance: the fact that a previous occupier of the affected land had not complained does not bind a subsequent occupier.

(iii) statutory authority: the defendant may have a defence where their actions are in pursuance of a statutory power or duty, though it seems they must take all reasonable steps to keep any nuisance caused to a minimum.

(f) remedies: at common law, a successful plaintiff has a right to damages. However, it may well be that the plaintiff wants the nuisance stopped by an injunction. It should be remembered that an injunction, being an equitable remedy, lies in the discretion of the court and will only be granted where it is just and equitable to do so. A self-help remedy, abatement, is also available. The plaintiff may take all reasonable steps to stop the nuisance though, for a variety of reasons, this is usually not advisable.

Public nuisance

A public nuisance is an act or omission which materially affects the comfort and convenience in life of a class of Her Majesty's subjects (*Attorney General v. PYA Quarries Ltd* (1957)). Therefore, the nuisance must affect an identifiable group of the general public. Accordingly, actions such as obstructing the highway, keeping a brothel and polluting the public water supply have been held to be public nuisances.

Public nuisance is essentially a crime and is tried on indictment in the Crown Court. Alternatively, either the Attorney General or the relevant local council may bring a civil *relator* action on behalf of the affected public.

Once the criminal or relator action has been proved, any individual who has suffered *special damage* (*i.e.* particular damage over and above that suffered by the public at large) may bring a civil action for damages (*Halsey v. Esso Petroleum Co Ltd* (1961)).

Statutory nuisance

Many activities have been effectively removed from the sphere of private nuisance as a result of a range of statutory provisions which grant wide powers to local authorities to take steps to prevent environmental damage. Thus, many forms of pollution (notably noise and smoke pollution) are now statutory nuisances under the Public Health Act 1936, the Clean Air Act 1956 and the Control of Pollution Act 1974.

d. Strict Liability in Tort

Liability in tort is generally dependent upon proof of fault on the part of the defendant. However, there is a limited amount of strict liability, principally concerning liability for certain extra-hazardous activities and justified on grounds of public policy. This liability may be imposed by statute (for example, the Nuclear Installations Act 1965, the Control of Pollution Act 1974) or under the common law rule established in *Rylands v. Fletcher* (1868).

Under the rule in *Rylands v. Fletcher*, a person who is in occupation of land and who brings onto that land something which is not naturally there, and does so for his own non-natural use, and that something is likely to do mischief should it escape, then that person will be liable for the consequences of any such escape, even in the absence of any fault on his part. The various elements of this rule require further explanation:

(a) the defendant must have been in occupation (*i.e.* in control) of the land from which the thing escapes.

(b) the thing must not have been naturally present on the land (for example, self-sown trees and plants are naturally present whereas deliberately cultivated ones are not).

(c) the thing must have been brought onto the land by the defendant for his own use, though not necessarily for his own benefit.

(d) the defendant must have been using the land in some non-natural way; *i.e.* he must have been engaged in some special use bringing with it an increased danger to others, and not merely the ordinary use of land or use which is for the general benefit of the community (*Rickards v. Lothian* (1913)). This considerably limits the scope of the rule in practice.

(e) the thing must be likely to do mischief should it escape. This does not mean the thing has to be inherently dangerous, merely that it is potentially dangerous should it escape in an uncontrolled way.

(f) the thing must escape, *i.e.* leave the confines of the defendant's land (*Read v. J. Lyons & Co Ltd* (1947)). Where there is no escape, the plaintiff must rely on the principles of negligence, occupiers' liability or nuisance as appropriate.

While liability under the rule is strict, it is not absolute, and there are five main defences which the defendant may invoke:

(a) the defendant is not liable where the escape is due to an Act of God. This applies where the escape is the result of natural causes without any human intervention, and such natural events were not reasonably foreseeable (*Tennent v. Earl of Glasgow* (1864)).

(b) the defendant may be able to avoid liability where he was acting under statutory authority.

(c) the defendant will not be liable where the escape is due to the unforeseeable act of a stranger (for example, a trespasser).

(d) the defendant will not be liable where the plaintiff had, expressly or impliedly, consented to the thing being brought onto the land or to its remaining there. Thus, while 'coming into' the situation is no defence to an action in nuisance, it may be a defence to an action based on the rule. Consent here means true consent, in the sense that the plaintiff was aware not only of the presence of the thing but also of its potential for mischief should it escape.

(e) the defendant will not be liable where the escape is due to the fault of the plaintiff. Where the escape is partly due to the fault of the plaintiff, contributory negligence will apply (see above).

Regarding remedies, the plaintiff will be able to claim damages in respect of all reasonably foreseeable consequences of the escape

(*Cambridge Water Co v. Eastern Counties Leather* (1993)). This allows recovery for personal injury, property damage and any consequential economic loss, but not for pure economic loss (*Cattle v. Stockton Waterworks Co* (1875)).

Given the various limitations and restrictions outlined above, it is probably best to think of the rule as a peculiar variation of the general law of nuisance, rather than as a significant form of liability in its own right (*Cambridge Water Co v. Eastern Counties Leather* (1993)).

e. Vicarious Liability

Vicarious liability is the term used to describe the situation where one person is liable for the torts of another by virtue of the relationship between them. By far the most common such relationship is that of employer and employee.

There are four main justifications for the imposition of strict liability in these circumstances:

(a) the employee's actions are generally at the instigation of the employer.

(b) the employee's actions are generally for the benefit of the employer.

(c) vicarious liability generally provides the plaintiff with a financially secure defendant.

(d) vicarious liability acts as an incentive to employers to select competent employees, to train them adequately and to establish safe working practices.

It follows from this that the employer's vicarious liability is a form of *enterprise* liability, limited to liabilities resulting from the conduct of his business. Therefore, in order for such liability to arise, two requirements must be met:

(a) **the relationship of employment:** there must be a relationship of employment between the 'employee' committing the tort and the 'employer'. The most obvious evidence of such a relationship would be a contract of employment. However, the relationship remains one for the courts, not the parties, to define. Therefore an express contractual provision that the relationship is not one of employment will not prevail over a preponderance of other terms and factors which indicate that it is (*Mersey Docks and Harbour Board v. Coggins and Griffiths (Liverpool) Ltd* (1947)).

In assessing whether, on balance, the relationship is one of employment, the courts may take into account a number of factors:

(i) the issue of control: where the 'employer' controls the type and manner of performance of the work of the 'employee', the relationship is likely to be one of employment.

(ii) the issue of integration: a person whose activities are integral to the enterprise (such as a ship's master or company chauffeur) is more likely to be regarded as an employee than someone whose activities are ancillary to the enterprise or temporarily attached to it (for example, the harbour pilot or hire car driver) (*Stevenson, Jordan and Harrison Ltd v. Macdonald* (1952)).

(iii) the method of payment (whether wages or salary or a lump sum), the responsibility for providing premises, materials and equipment, and any provisions for disciplinary measures and dismissal (*Mersey Docks and Harbour Board v. Coggins and Griffiths (Liverpool) Ltd* (1947)).

The plaintiff does not have to identify the particular employee responsible *provided* it is clear that the tort must have been committed by one of the defendant's employees (*Grant v. Australian Knitting Mills Ltd* (1936)).

(b) **the tort must have been committed in the course of employment:** this means the employee must have committed the tort while performing work he was employed to do at the time he was employed to do it. This includes the improper performance of work employed to do (*Century Insurance Co Ltd v. Northern Ireland Road Transport Board* (1942)).

Therefore, an express prohibition by the employer regarding the *manner* of performance will not, in itself, take an act in breach of that prohibition outside the course of employment (*Limpus v. London General Omnibus Co* (1862)). By contrast, a prohibition regarding the *type* of work to be performed will normally take an act in breach of that prohibition outside the course of employment (*Iqbal v. London Transport Executive* (1973)).

The fact that the employee's conduct is also criminal will not necessarily take it outside the course of employment: the employer may remain liable where the criminal act was an improper performance of work employed to do (*Lloyd v. Grace, Smith & Co* (1912)).

(c) The position of the independent contractor: it follows from the above that an employer will not normally be liable for the acts of an independent contractor. However, the employer may be liable where the contractor is in breach of a *non-delegable duty* binding on the employer. In such circumstances, while the employer can delegate performance of the duty to a contractor, he cannot delegate the duty itself and will remain personally (*not* vicariously) liable should the contractor breach that duty.

A non-delegable duty may arise in two main circumstances:
   (i) where the commissioned work involves exceptional risk to others. Here the employer will be liable for any negligence by the contractor inthe performance of that work (*Holliday v. National Telephone Co* (1899)) but not for any collateral negligence (*Padbury v. Holliday and Greenwood Ltd* (1912)).
  (ii) where the employer owes the victim a duty of care for their safety and protection (for example, the duty on employers to provide for the health and safety at work of their employees; *Smith v. Cammell Laird & Co Ltd* (1940); the duty on Healh Authorities and hospitals for the welfare and safety of patients in their care; *Cassidy v. Ministry of Health* (1951)).

f. The Role of Fault in Tort

The aim of the law of tort is to provide a remedy (usually in the form of financial compensation) for the victims of wrongs, and fault on the part of the defendant is the device most generally used to attach liability for such compensation. However, while there are clear arguments in favour of a fault-based system of liability, the present insistence on proof of fault places significant and often insurmountable obstacles in the path of the very people the system is designed to benefit. This has given rise to increasing concerns, particularly in relation to personal injury cases.

The arguments in favour of fault-based liability

There are four main arguments for retention of a fault based system:

(a) it is a just approach to the apportioning of liability. Where fault indicates the person responsible for the damage, justice requires that the person compensate the victim. However, it is questionable whether justice requires that, in the absence of fault, the loss should be borne by the blameless victim.

(b) the requirement of fault acts as an incentive to take care, since if liability were imposed regardless of fault, people would take less care because no advantage would accrue to the careful. However, this argument rests on the rather dubious assumption that people take care to avoid injuring others solely or largely in order to avoid legal liability.

(c) the requirement of fault deters deliberate self-maiming. It is true that in jurisdictions with no-fault systems there have been instances of people injuring themselves in order to obtain compensation. However, the numbers currently denied access to compensation by the requirement of fault far exceed any likely number of self-maiming claims. Furthermore, it should be possible to build safeguards into a no-fault system to deal with such cases.

(d) to move to a no-fault system would involve a massive extension of liability and place an excessive burden on defendants. Whether this would in fact result would depend upon how the system was funded, but even under the present arrangements the bulk of any additional costs would be spread throughout society at large, through a rise in insurance costs, rather than falling directly upon individuals.

The arguments against fault-based liability

There are two main arguments against the retention of a fault-based system:

(a) the practical consequences of a fault-based system are unacceptable. The difficulties in establishing both fault and causation make the system a 'forensic lottery'. Furthermore, it is an extremely inefficient mechanism for compensation.

The Pearson Commission (which reported in 1978) found that the administrative costs of the tort system were equivalent to 85 per cent of the sums paid in compensation, amounting to 45 per cent of the total compensation and administration costs. By contrast, compensation via the social security system would involve administration costs amounting to only 11 per cent of the total, thereby providing a substantially cheaper and quicker compensation mechanism.

(b) a fault-based system is wrong in principle as well as practice. While fault may provide a good reason for taking money from defendants, it is an inappropriate basis on which to decide which victims will receive compensation. Furthermore, except where there is joint liability or contributory negligence, the present system takes no account of the *degree* of fault. Thus, an act of momentary carelessness which results in serious damage will give rise to far greater liability than an act of gross negligence which results in only minor harm. Also, because the aim is to compensate the victim, the assessment of damages takes no account of the defendant's ability to pay (unlike the criminal law when assessing the level of fines). Finally, it may be argued that the present system has itself recognised these failings by allowing (and even in some cases making compulsory) the use of loss-distribution devices such as insurance and developing notions such as vicarious liability.

The main alternative—a no-fault system

The main alternative to the use of a fault-based tort system for the compensation of accident victims is the introduction of a no-fault compensation system (such as that in New Zealand), financed either through compulsory private insurance or public revenues. Critics of such schemes often point to the fact that the levels of compensation available fall below those provided by damages at common law. However, the fact remains that a system which ensures adequate compensation for all would seem to be preferable to the continuation of a system which provides full compensation for only a few.

Section Seven: ANSWERING QUESTIONS

1. ESSAY WRITING

The most important thing to remember when answering an essay question is to ensure you answer the *specific* question set, and *not* merely recite a stock answer or write all you can remember about the particular topic concerned.

It is also essential to **PLAN** your answer carefully before you begin. This is true *both* of homework *and* timed or examination essays. A clear plan is vital to ensure relevance, accuracy, clarity and logical argument.

Generally, an 'A' Level essay should have three main parts:

(a) Introduction

This should state what you understand the question to be asking. You should *not* do this by simply re-writing the question in your own words. Rather you should indicate the *issues* and *ideas* the question is raising, providing a context for the discussion that will follow.

Thus, the introduction provides a 'gateway' to the main part of the essay. This function can be helped by finishing the introduction with a *link statement*, indicating to the reader what will follow. It may be useful to use the language of the question itself in constructing this statement. This will help to ensure relevance, to show you are in control of your knowledge and that you are seeking to answer the particular question set.

(b) Description and Evaluation

'A' Level questions generally require *both* description *and* evaluation. Where the question is set in a two-part format, it is likely that part (a) requires description and (b) evaluation.

It is important that in this part of the essay you develop your arguments in a clear and logical manner. This again emphasises the need for a good plan. A fairly typical structure might be:

- the law at present—describe
    —evaluate (advantages and disadvantages)
    —how satisfactory is this?
- possible reforms —describe
    —evaluate
    —which, if any, are desirable?

(c) Conclusion

This should draw together the various arguments you have developed in the main part of the essay into a coherent overall response to the question set. It should follow logically from the preceding discussion and *not* come as a surprise to the reader (again emphasising the need for a good plan).

Two more general points

(a) remember the **THREE Cs**: be **CONCISE**
    be **CLEAR**
    be **CORRECT**

You will only be able to score highly under the time constraints of the examination by ensuring you are able to communicate accurate knowledge and understanding in a clear and concise style.

(b) when citing authorities, try to give a brief description of the relevant facts, for example:

(*Olley v. Marlborough Court Ltd* (1949): exclusion notice in hotel bedroom not incorporated as contract made in reception).

Remember that the citing of authorities should be used to support arguments or propositions you have already clearly and concisely stated.

(d) An Example Essay

Critically evaluate the statutory schemes for civil legal aid, advice and representation.

Plan

Introduction	—importance of access —inequality of access (unmet need) LINK (use language of question)
Description	—1949 Act (3 elements) —advice and assistance—Green Form (1972) ————————————————————————means test only ————————————————————————ABWOR (1979) —aid (means and merits test)
Evaluation	—only tackles cost barrier —cost-effective? —eligibility (middle income trap) —second class service —unavailability (eg. tribunals)
Conclusion	—subsidies alone no answer —combine with professional diversification and alternative/complementary provision (CABx, *etc.*) —shift of resources

Under the rule of law, all citizens are equal. However, this principle only has practical meaning if all citizens have adequate access to the institutions that uphold it. Therefore, equal access to legal services is fundamental in ensuring all citizens benefit from the protection of law. However, this equality does not exist. Rather, there is an unmet need for legal services. In the 1970s, Abel-Smith, Zander and Brooke identified three forms of unmet need: first, where someone does not recognise their problem as a legal one; secondly, where the problem is recognised as legal, but they are unable to access the available services; thirdly, where the problem is recognised, but no appropriate help exists. According to Harris, there are four main barriers which prevent many people accessing legal services: an imbalance in geographical availability; reluctance to get involved with the law; inadequate knowledge of some areas

of law among practitioners; and the high cost of private legal services. It is now necessary to critically evaluate the statutory
schemes designed to overcome this unmet need with regard to civil
matters.

State funding of legal services was introduced by the Legal Aid
and Advice Act 1949. This was intended to provide access in three
ways. First, by subsidising the cost of litigation and representation
(legal aid). Secondly, by subsidising preliminary and non-
contentious work (advice and assistance). Thirdly, by establishing
a public solicitor service (this was never done).

Funding for legal advice and representation was not in fact introduced until the Legal Advice and Assistance Act 1972 established
the 'Green Form' scheme. This allows solicitors to do a small
amount of cash-limited work (such as initial advice, writing letters,
drafitng documents, *etc.*) for those who qualify under a means test.
The Legal Aid Act 1979 extended the scheme to cover limited
forms of representation (for example, before the Mental Health
Review Tribunal). This is known as Assistance By Way Of Representation (ABWOR).

To qualify for legal aid for civil litigation and representation, the
applicant must satisfy both a means and merits test. The means
test involves an assessment of the applicant's disposable income.
Where this is above a certain level, aid will not be available. Where
below a certain level, full aid may be granted. Where between these
two levels, some aid may be granted with the applicant making a
graduated contribution. The merits test requires the applicant to
show they have reasonable grounds for taking, defending or being
a party to the proceedings in question.

These statutory schemes, while they have undoubtedly made
some contribution to increasing access, have been subject to a
number of criticisms. First, the schemes only address one of the
barriers to access, cost. Any strategy that only tackles part of the
problem can only ever be part of the solution. Secondly, they are
not very cost-effective. There is a dilemma between ever-increasing
costs and cutbacks in the level of provision. In fact, while costs have
steadily risen (to over £1 billion per year), the proportion of the
population eligible has fallen from approximately two-thirds in
1979 to around one-third in 1991. Thirdly, this decline in eligibility
has resulted in the 'middle income trap', where a large proportion
of the population is not eligible for aid but cannot afford to pay for
legal services themselves. Fourthly, some claim that legally-aided
clients often receive a second class service when compared to that
offered to private, fee-paying clients. Finally, with the growth of

alternative methods of dispute resolution (such as tribunals), concerns have been expressed that legal aid is rarely available in these circumstances.

Therefore, it seems that the statutory schemes alone offer no long-term answer to the problems of access to civil legal aid, advice and representation. There must be a combination of subsidies with professional diversification (possibly aided by the introduction of contingency fees and growth in private legal insurance) and alternative and complementary providers (such as CABx and Law Centres). Furthermore, any such broad strategy would seem to require a shift of resources away from reliance on subsidies and towards a comprehensive and properly funded network of complementary provision.

2. PROBLEM ANSWERING

In answering 'problem' style questions, you should consider using the following approach:

(1) read the facts and all the questions carefully: use the questions to help you identify the relevant issues and facts.
(2) list the important and relevant facts, in the order in which they happen, together with the issue(s) each raises in a **'facts and issues table'**.
(3) write mini-plans for each question, identifying the main issue(s) and relevant facts.
(4) answer each question in full, referring to the mini-plans and facts and issues table, using the **'three stage approach'**:
   (a) **identify** and **define** the issues raised.
   (b) **state** and **explain** the relevant **rules** of law (with **authorities**).
   (c) **apply** the **rules** to the **facts** and **suggest** the likely outcome.

An Example Problem

Ann goes to Brian's Hardware Store to buy a new pump for her central heating system. She explains her requirements to Brian, who sells her a pump he assures her is suitable. Ann subsequently discovers that the pump is far too powerful for use with her system. However, when she complains to Brian, he claims there is nothing he can do, pointing out a statement on the invoice Ann received when buying the pump, which states that the Hardware Store has no liability for defective or unsuitable producs.

(a) Explain the terms of the contract between Ann and Brian and consider which, if any, have been broken.

(b) Assuming the contract has been broken, consider the significance of the statement on the invoice for Brian's liability.

Facts	Issues
1) A goes to B to buy pump	Sale of goods
2) A explains requirements and B assures her pump is suitable	s.14(3)
3) A discovers pump is not suitable	Breach
4) B refuses to do anything, pointing to clause on invoice	Exclusion clause

Mini-plans

(a) issue = terms (especially SOGA '79) and breach
  facts: 1,2,3

(b) issue = exclusion clause
  facts: 4

(a) This question raises the issue of the terms of the contract between Ann and Brian and whether any have been broken. It is the terms of the contract that define the rights and duties of the parties to it. These will be made up of express terms (those actually stated by the parties themselves, such as the price to be paid) and implied terms (those implied into the contract by common law or statute). Of particular relevance here are the implied terms under the Sale of Goods Act 1979 (as amended by the Sale and Supply of Goods Act 1994). The rules of law relating to these issues must now be explained.

The 1979 Act applies to all contracts for the sale of goods. Section 2 defines these as contracts where the ownership of goods is exchanged for money. The Act then implies up to four important terms into such contracts. Section 12 implies into all contracts for the sale of goods a condition that the seller has the right to sell the goods. Section 13 provides that where the sale is a sale by description, there is a condition that the goods must correspond with that description (for example, a coat described as '100 per cent pure new wool' must in fact be 100 per cent pure new wool). Section 14 only applies where the seller is selling in the course of a business. Section 14(2) implies a general requirement that the goods be of satisfactory quality. Section 14(2B) provides that 'quality' includes not only functional characteristics (such as fitness for common purpose, freedom from minor defects, safety and durability) but also cosmetic characteristics (such as appearance and finish), together with the general state and condition of the goods. However, under section 14(2C), this requirement does not apply to defects specifically drawn to the buyer's attention at or before the time of sale, or to defects which a reasonable examination would have revealed (provided the buyer did in fact examine the goods before the contract was made). This general requirement refers only to goods being fit for their common purpose. However, section 14(3) provides that where the buyer informs the seller of any particular purpose (whether common or not) for which the goods are being bought, then the goods must be fit for that purpose unless the seller can show either that the buyer did not rely on the seller's skill and judgment or that such reliance was unreasonable in the circumstances. Finally, section 15 provides that where the sale is a sale by sample, there is a condition that the bulk must correspond with the sample in quality.

Applying the rules outlined above to the facts as given, the contract between Ann and Brian is one for the sale of goods and is, therefore, subject to the provisions of the 1979 Act. Ann informed Brian of the particular purpose for which she was buying the pump, and Brian assured her the pump was suitable. In the circumstances, it seems that Ann did reasonably rely on Brian's skill and judgment. Therefore, given that Brian is selling in the course of a business, it seems that he is in breach of the implied condition under section 14(3) because he has sold Ann a pump which is unfit for the particular purpose.

(b) This question raises the issue of exclusion clauses and whether Brian can rely on the statement on the invoice to avoid liability for breach of contract. An exclusion clause is a term of the contract which seeks to limit or exclude liability for breach of contract. While such clauses are perfectly legitimate in theory, they may be misused in practice by parties in a dominant bargaining position (particularly when included in standard form contracts). Therefore, their use is subject to both judicial and statutory regulation. The rules of law relating to this issue must now be explained.

The courts have developed two main controls over the use of exclusion clauses. First, the clause must have been properly incorporated into the contract. This means the other party must have been given reasonably sufficient notice of the clause (*Parker v. South Eastern Railway Co* (1877)) at or before the time the contract was made (*Olley v. Marlborough Court Ltd* (1949); *Thornton v. Shoe Lane Parking* (1971)). Secondly, upon proper construction (or interpretation) the clause must cover the breach that has occurred. In construing exclusion clauses, the courts are guided by two presumptions. First, under the *contra proferentem* rule, any doubt or ambiguity in the clause is construed against the party seeking to rely on it (*i.e.* the benefit of any doubt is given to the injured party) (*Baldry v. Marshall* (1925); *Andrews v. Singer* (1934)). Secondly, under the main purpose rule, it is presumed no exclusion clause is intended to exclude liability for failing to perform the main purpose of the contract (*Glynn v. Margetson & Co* (1893)). However, this presumption may be rebutted by sufficiently strong and clear words (*Suisse Atlantique* (1967); *Photo Production Ltd v. Securicor Transport Ltd* (1980)). Turning to statutory regulation, the Unfair Contract Terms Act 1977 invalidates the use of exclusion clauses in some circumstances and subjects them to a strict test of reasonableness in others. Section 6 regulates attempts to exclude or restrict liability for breach of the implied terms under the 1979 Act. Liability for breach of the implied condition as to title (s.12, 1979) cannot be excluded or restricted in any circumstances. Liability for breach of the implied conditions as to correspondence with description (s.13, 1979), satisfactory quality (s.14, 1979) and correspondence with sample (s.15, 1979) cannot be excluded or restricted as against a consumer, and only as against a non-consumer in so far as the term is reasonable. Section 12 of the 1977 Act defines a consumer as someone who is not dealing in the course of a business contracting with someone who is. Where the contract is one for the sale of goods, there is an additional requirement that the goods are of a type that is usually supplied for private use or consumption.

Applying the rules outlined above to the facts as given, it would seem that the clause on the invoice is likely to pass the incorporation and construction tests. However, as Ann seems to fall within the definition of a consumer, any attempt to exclude or restrict liability for breach of the implied condition under s.14(3) of the1979 Act will be invalid by virtue of section 6 of the 1977 Act. Therefore, it appears that Brian cannot rely on the clause to escape his liability for breach of contract.

INDEX